Axton Nexus

Computer Graphics Development With Vulkan

A Hands-On Beginner's Guide to Building
High-Quality, Real-Time 3D Graphics
Applications for Games, Simulations, and
Visualizations

Table Of Content

Disclaimer

The information provided in this book, "Computer Graphics Development With Vulkan: A Hands-On Beginner's Guide," is intended for educational and informational purposes only. While every effort has been made to ensure the accuracy and completeness of[1] the content, the author and publisher make no representations or warranties of any kind, express or implied, about the completeness, accuracy, reliability,[2] suitability, or availability with respect to the book or the information, products, services, or related graphics contained in the book for any purpose. Any reliance you place on such information is therefore strictly at your own risk.[3]

The code examples and techniques presented in this book are intended to illustrate concepts and provide a starting point for your own Vulkan development. They may not be suitable for all situations or production environments and may require modification or adaptation to meet your specific needs. The author and publisher are not responsible for any errors, omissions, or damages that may result from the use of the code or techniques described in this book.

Vulkan is a complex and evolving API, and its implementation and behavior may vary across different hardware vendors and driver versions. The author and publisher are not responsible for any compatibility issues or performance variations that may arise from using Vulkan on different platforms or configurations.

This book is not affiliated with or endorsed by the Khronos Group, the developers of Vulkan. All trademarks and registered trademarks mentioned in this book are the property of their respective owners.

The author and publisher reserve the right to make changes to the content of this book at any time without notice.

Limitations of Liability

In no event will the author or publisher be liable for any loss or damage including without limitation, indirect or consequential loss or damage, or any[4] loss or damage whatsoever arising from loss of data or profits arising out of, or in connection with, the use of this[5] book.

External Links

This book may contain links to external websites that are not provided or maintained by the author or publisher. The author and publisher do not have any control over the content of those sites and are not responsible for the availability, accuracy, or suitability of any information found there. The inclusion of any links does not necessarily imply a recommendation or endorse the views expressed within them.

Copyright[6]

The content of this book is protected by copyright law. No part of this book may be reproduced, distributed, or transmitted in any form or by any means, including photocopying,[7] recording, or other electronic or mechanical methods, without the prior written permission of the publisher, except in the case of brief quotations embodied in critical reviews and certain other[8] noncommercial uses permitted by copyright law.[9]

Introduction

In the ever-evolving landscape of computer graphics, Vulkan has emerged as a powerful and versatile graphics API, offering developers unprecedented control and efficiency in harnessing the capabilities of modern GPUs. This book, "Computer Graphics Development With Vulkan: A Hands-On Beginner's Guide," invites you to explore the exciting world of Vulkan and embark on a rewarding journey to master the art of creating high-quality, real-time 3D graphics applications.

Whether you're an aspiring game developer, a simulation enthusiast, or a visualization expert, this book provides a comprehensive and accessible introduction to Vulkan, guiding you through the fundamentals and progressively introducing more advanced techniques. With a hands-on approach, you'll learn by doing, building practical examples and tackling engaging challenges that solidify your understanding and empower you to create your own stunning visuals.

Why Vulkan?

Vulkan's popularity stems from its distinct advantages over traditional graphics APIs:

- **Unleashed Performance:** Vulkan's streamlined architecture and reduced overhead empower you to extract maximum performance from your hardware, achieving higher frame rates and smoother experiences.

- **Explicit Control:** Vulkan grants you fine-grained control over the graphics pipeline, allowing you to optimize rendering for your specific needs and achieve unique visual effects.
- **Cross-Platform Compatibility:** Vulkan's cross-platform nature ensures your applications can run seamlessly across a variety of devices and operating systems, from powerful PCs to mobile devices.
- **Future-Proof Technology:** As the successor to OpenGL, Vulkan represents the future of graphics APIs, equipping you with the skills and knowledge to create cutting-edge applications for years to come.

What You'll Learn

This book covers a wide range of topics, starting with the fundamentals of Vulkan and progressing to advanced rendering techniques and real-world applications:

- **Vulkan Basics:** Master the core concepts of Vulkan, including instance creation, device management, memory allocation, and command buffer submission.

- **Graphics Pipeline:** Understand the stages of the Vulkan graphics pipeline, from vertex processing and tessellation to fragment shading and output merging.
- **Shaders:** Learn to write vertex and fragment shaders in GLSL, the shading language used in Vulkan, and explore advanced shader techniques like tessellation and geometry shaders.
- **Textures and Samplers:** Discover how to utilize textures to add detail and realism to your scenes, and master the art of sampling and filtering textures for optimal visual quality.
- **Advanced Rendering:** Explore advanced rendering techniques like deferred shading, screen-space ambient occlusion, and shadow mapping to create stunning visual effects.
- **Performance Optimization:** Learn to profile and optimize your Vulkan applications for peak performance, utilizing techniques like batching, instancing, and efficient shader coding.
- **Real-World Applications:** Apply your Vulkan knowledge to build real-world applications, including a simple game engine, a 3D visualization tool, and a virtual reality experience.

Who Should Read This Book

This book is tailored for:

- **Aspiring Game Developers:** Those eager to learn a powerful and modern graphics API for creating cutting-edge games.
- **Simulation Enthusiasts:** Individuals interested in building realistic simulations and visualizing complex data.
- **Visualization Experts:** Professionals seeking to leverage Vulkan's capabilities for high-performance and interactive visualizations.
- **Graphics Programmers:** Developers looking to expand their skillset and embrace the future of graphics APIs.

Prerequisites

While this book is designed for beginners, some familiarity with basic programming concepts and C++ will be beneficial. No prior experience with graphics APIs is required.

A Hands-On Approach

This book emphasizes a hands-on learning approach. Throughout the chapters, you'll find practical examples, code snippets, and engaging challenges that encourage you to apply your knowledge and build your own Vulkan applications.

Embark on Your Vulkan Adventure

With its comprehensive coverage, clear explanations, and practical examples, this book equips you with the tools and knowledge to confidently navigate the world of Vulkan. So, open your mind, embrace the challenge, and get ready to unleash your creativity as you embark on this exciting adventure into the realm of high-performance graphics programming.

Part I: Foundations

Chapter 1: Introduction to Vulkan and Modern Graphics

The Evolution of Graphics APIs

The journey of computer graphics is a fascinating tale of innovation, driven by the relentless pursuit of realism and performance. At the heart of this journey lie Graphics APIs (Application Programming Interfaces), the crucial bridges connecting software with the hardware that brings our digital worlds to life. This evolution has been marked by significant shifts in design philosophy, mirroring the advancements in GPU technology and the increasing demands of visual applications.

Early Days: Fixed-Function Pipelines

In the nascent years of computer graphics, developers worked with **fixed-function pipelines**. These APIs, like the early versions of OpenGL, provided a predefined set of operations for rendering graphics. Think of it like a factory assembly line with fixed stations: data would flow through a rigid sequence of transformations, lighting, and rasterization steps. While this simplified development, it severely limited flexibility and control over the rendering process.

The Rise of Programmable Shaders

The introduction of **programmable shaders** revolutionized graphics programming. With languages like GLSL (OpenGL Shading Language) and HLSL (High-Level Shading Language), developers gained the power to write custom programs that execute directly on the GPU. This unlocked unprecedented control over the graphics pipeline, enabling a vast array of visual effects and rendering techniques.

Imagine now that you could reconfigure the factory assembly line at will, adding new stations, changing their order, and customizing their operations. This is the power that shaders brought to graphics development.

The Need for Modern APIs

As GPUs became more powerful and parallel architectures evolved, the limitations of older APIs became apparent. They were designed for an era of single-core CPUs and simpler hardware. This led to performance bottlenecks and hindered developers from fully harnessing the capabilities of modern GPUs.

This demand for efficiency and control gave rise to modern graphics APIs like **Vulkan**, **DirectX 12**, and **Metal**. These APIs are characterized by:

- **Explicit Control:** They give developers more direct control over GPU resources and operations, reducing driver overhead and allowing for finer-grained optimization.
- **Reduced CPU Overhead:** They minimize the burden on the CPU, enabling it to focus on other tasks like game logic and physics simulations.
- **Multi-threading:** They are designed to exploit the parallelism of modern CPUs, allowing for efficient distribution of rendering tasks across multiple cores.

Vulkan: A Modern Graphics Powerhouse

Vulkan, developed by the Khronos Group, stands out as a truly cross-platform, high-performance graphics API. It provides a thin layer of abstraction over the underlying hardware, offering exceptional control and efficiency. This makes it ideal for demanding applications like:

- **AAA Games:** Pushing the boundaries of visual fidelity and performance.
- **Simulations:** Rendering complex scientific and engineering data.
- **Virtual Reality (VR):** Creating immersive and responsive VR experiences.

The Future of Graphics APIs

The evolution of graphics APIs continues. New extensions and features are constantly being added to address emerging technologies like ray tracing and machine learning. With the rise of WebGPU, high-performance graphics are even making their way to the web.

By understanding the evolution of graphics APIs, you gain a deeper appreciation for the tools and techniques that shape the digital world around us. This knowledge provides a solid foundation for mastering Vulkan and embarking on your journey to create stunning, high-performance graphics applications.

Why Vulkan? Advantages and Use Cases

Vulkan has rapidly become a game-changer in the world of graphics APIs, offering a compelling blend of power, efficiency, and control. Let's delve into the key advantages that make Vulkan a preferred choice for developers seeking to push the boundaries of graphical fidelity and performance.

1. Unleashing Performance: Reduced Overhead

Traditional graphics APIs often introduce significant overhead due to layers of abstraction and driver management. Vulkan, in contrast, adopts a "thin driver" approach, minimizing CPU intervention and allowing developers to communicate more directly with the GPU. This translates to:

- **Reduced CPU Load:** Vulkan streamlines the rendering process, freeing up the CPU for other critical tasks like physics calculations, AI, and game logic.
- **Increased Frame Rates:** By optimizing resource management and minimizing bottlenecks, Vulkan can deliver smoother and more responsive graphics performance.
- **Lower Power Consumption:** Efficient utilization of GPU resources can lead to reduced power consumption, especially beneficial for mobile and embedded devices.

2. Explicit Control: The Power of Choice

Vulkan empowers developers with explicit control over various aspects of the rendering process. This fine-grained control enables:

- **Customized Rendering Pipelines:** Developers can tailor the rendering pipeline to their specific needs, optimizing for performance or specific visual effects.
- **Memory Management:** Vulkan provides direct control over memory allocation and usage, allowing for efficient resource utilization and minimizing memory waste.

- **Synchronization:** Precise control over synchronization mechanisms ensures optimal execution of rendering tasks and prevents data hazards.

3. Cross-Platform Compatibility

Vulkan is designed to be truly cross-platform, supporting a wide range of operating systems and hardware platforms, including:

- **Desktop:** Windows, Linux, macOS
- **Mobile:** Android, iOS
- **Embedded Systems:** Consoles, IoT devices

This portability allows developers to reach a broader audience with their applications and reduces the need for platform-specific code.

4. A Versatile API: Beyond Graphics

While Vulkan excels in graphics rendering, its capabilities extend beyond traditional graphics tasks. It also supports:

- **Compute Shaders:** Leveraging the GPU for general-purpose parallel computing tasks like physics simulations, image processing, and machine learning.

- **Asynchronous Compute:** Overlapping graphics and compute workloads for increased efficiency and utilization of GPU resources.

Use Cases: Where Vulkan Shines

Vulkan's unique advantages make it an ideal choice for a variety of demanding applications:

- **High-Performance Games:** AAA game developers are increasingly adopting Vulkan to achieve stunning visuals and smooth frame rates.
- **Virtual Reality (VR):** Vulkan's low latency and efficient rendering are crucial for creating immersive and responsive VR experiences.
- **Simulations and Scientific Visualization:** Vulkan can handle the complex data sets and rendering demands of scientific simulations and visualizations.
- **Mobile and Embedded Devices:** Vulkan's efficiency and cross-platform compatibility make it well-suited for resource-constrained devices.

As you delve deeper into Vulkan, you'll discover how its features and capabilities can be harnessed to create cutting-edge graphics applications that push the boundaries of visual innovation.

Key Concepts and Terminology

Before we begin working with Vulkan, it's essential to establish a shared understanding of its core concepts and terminology. This foundation will help you navigate the API and grasp the logic behind its design.

1. Vulkan Objects:

Vulkan revolves around a collection of objects, each representing a specific component or resource within the graphics system. These objects are typically created and managed by the application. Some fundamental Vulkan objects include:

- **Instance:** The root object representing your application's connection to the Vulkan library.
- **Physical Device:** Represents a physical GPU in your system.
- **Logical Device:** An abstraction of the physical device, through which you interact with the GPU.
- **Queues:** Handles for submitting commands to the GPU for execution.
- **Buffers:** Memory blocks used to store various types of data, such as vertex attributes, indices, and uniform variables.
- **Images:** Represent textures and render targets.
- **Shaders:** Programs that run on the GPU to process graphics data.

- **Pipeline:** A sequence of operations that define how graphics data is processed and rendered.

2. Vulkan Functions:

Vulkan's functionality is exposed through a set of functions that allow you to create, manipulate, and destroy Vulkan objects, as well as submit commands to the GPU. These functions typically follow a consistent naming convention (e.g., vkCreateInstance, vkAllocateMemory, vkCmdDraw).

3. Validation Layers:

Vulkan provides optional validation layers that act as debugging tools, helping you identify potential errors or incorrect API usage during development. These layers can be invaluable for catching issues early on and ensuring your application adheres to Vulkan's specifications.

4. Vulkan Extensions:

Vulkan's core functionality can be extended through optional extensions, which provide access to additional features or platform-specific capabilities. Extensions allow Vulkan to adapt to evolving hardware and software environments.

5. The Vulkan Instance:

The Vulkan instance serves as the entry point to the API. It represents your application's connection to the Vulkan library and allows you to query available Vulkan devices and extensions.

6. Physical and Logical Devices:

- **Physical Device:** Represents a physical GPU in your system. You can query its properties, capabilities, and supported features.
- **Logical Device:** Created from a physical device, it acts as the interface through which you interact with the GPU and submit commands.

7. Queues and Command Buffers:

- **Queues:** Handles for submitting work to the GPU. Different queues may be dedicated to specific types of work (graphics, compute, transfer).
- **Command Buffers:** Containers that hold a sequence of commands to be executed by the GPU.

8. Synchronization:

Vulkan provides mechanisms for synchronizing operations within the GPU and between the CPU and GPU. This ensures correct execution order and prevents data races.

9. Swapchain:

The swapchain manages the presentation of rendered images to the display. It involves a set of buffers that are swapped to create smooth animation.

10. SPIR-V:

SPIR-V (Standard Portable Intermediate Representation - V) is the intermediate language used for Vulkan shaders. Shaders written in GLSL or HLSL are typically compiled to SPIR-V before being used in a Vulkan application.

By familiarizing yourself with these key concepts and terminology, you'll be well-prepared to explore the world of Vulkan and begin building your own high-performance graphics applications.

Setting Up Your Development Environment

Before you start writing Vulkan code, it's essential to set up a proper development environment on your system. This involves installing the necessary tools and libraries, configuring your IDE, and ensuring you have the right drivers.

1. Choose Your Operating System and Hardware

Vulkan is designed to be cross-platform, so you have the flexibility to work on Windows, Linux, or macOS. Ensure your hardware, especially your graphics card, supports Vulkan. You can usually find this information on the manufacturer's website.

2. Install the Vulkan SDK

The Vulkan SDK (Software Development Kit) provides the essential tools and libraries for Vulkan development. You can download the latest SDK from the official Vulkan website (vulkan.org). The SDK includes:

- **Vulkan Headers:** Contain the definitions for Vulkan functions, structures, and enumerations.
- **Vulkan Loader:** Dynamically loads the appropriate Vulkan driver for your graphics card.
- **Validation Layers:** Provide debugging and error checking during development.
- **Vulkan Tools:** Useful utilities for debugging, profiling, and analyzing Vulkan applications.

3. Set Up Your IDE

While you can technically write Vulkan code in any text editor, using an Integrated Development Environment (IDE) can significantly enhance your productivity. Popular choices for Vulkan development include:

- **Visual Studio:** A powerful IDE with excellent support for C++ and debugging.
- **CLion:** A cross-platform IDE with a focus on C++ development.
- **VS Code:** A lightweight and versatile code editor with extensive extensions for various programming languages.

Configure your chosen IDE to include the Vulkan header directories and link against the Vulkan libraries. This allows your IDE to understand Vulkan code and provide code completion and error highlighting.

4. Install a Build System

A build system automates the process of compiling and linking your Vulkan code. Commonly used build systems include:

- **CMake:** A cross-platform build system that generates project files for various IDEs.
- **Premake:** Another cross-platform build system with a focus on simplicity.

5. Verify Your Setup

Once you have installed the necessary components, it's crucial to verify that your setup is working correctly. The Vulkan SDK often includes sample programs that you can build and run to confirm that Vulkan is functioning as expected.

6. Choose a Graphics Library (Optional)

While Vulkan provides low-level access to the GPU, you might consider using a higher-level graphics library to simplify certain tasks and reduce boilerplate code. Popular choices include:

- **GLFW:** A multi-platform library for window creation, input handling, and OpenGL context management (also works with Vulkan).
- **SDL:** A cross-platform multimedia library that provides windowing, graphics rendering, audio playback, and input handling.
- **glm:** A header-only library for linear algebra operations commonly used in graphics programming.

7. Stay Updated

The world of graphics is constantly evolving. Keep your Vulkan SDK, drivers, and libraries up to date to take advantage of the latest features and performance improvements.

By carefully setting up your development environment, you'll create a solid foundation for your Vulkan projects and ensure a smooth and productive development experience.

Chapter 2: Vulkan Fundamentals

Instance and Physical Devices

In Vulkan, your interaction with the graphics hardware begins with the creation of a Vulkan instance and the identification of suitable physical devices. These initial steps are crucial for establishing a connection to the Vulkan API and selecting the GPU that will power your application.

The Vulkan Instance: Your Application's Gateway

The Vulkan instance serves as the primary point of contact between your application and the Vulkan library. It's the first object you create and acts as a handle for accessing Vulkan's functionalities. Think of it as the foundation upon which you'll build your graphics application.

Creating a Vulkan instance involves specifying certain application-level information, such as:

- **Application Name and Version:** Helps in identifying your application during debugging and profiling.
- **Engine Name and Version:** If you're using a game engine, providing this information can be useful for compatibility and support.

- **Required Vulkan API Version:** Ensures that your application uses the intended version of Vulkan.
- **Enabled Layers:** Specifies any optional validation layers you want to enable for debugging and error checking.
- **Enabled Extensions:** Specifies any optional extensions required by your application.

Once created, the Vulkan instance provides a gateway to discover and interact with the physical devices available in your system.

Physical Devices: Discovering Your GPUs

A physical device represents a physical GPU in your system. It could be a dedicated graphics card, an integrated graphics processor, or even a software-based Vulkan implementation. Vulkan allows you to enumerate the available physical devices and query their properties to determine their suitability for your application.

Important properties of a physical device include:

- **Device Name and Type:** Provides information about the GPU vendor and model.
- **API Version:** Indicates the highest Vulkan API version supported by the device.

- **Memory Properties:** Describes the different types of memory heaps available on the device and their characteristics.
- **Limits:** Specifies various limits of the device, such as maximum texture size, number of samplers, and buffer sizes.
- **Features:** Indicates the optional features supported by the device, such as geometry shaders, tessellation, and texture compression.
- **Queues:** Describes the queues supported by the device, which are used for submitting commands to the GPU.

Selecting the Right Physical Device

Choosing the appropriate physical device is crucial for optimizing your application's performance. Consider the following factors when making your selection:

- **Required Features:** Ensure the device supports all the Vulkan features required by your application.
- **Performance Characteristics:** Consider the device's memory capacity, clock speed, and compute power.
- **Power Consumption:** If power efficiency is a concern, choose a device with lower power consumption.

- **Dedicated vs. Integrated:** Dedicated graphics cards generally offer better performance, while integrated GPUs are more power-efficient.

By carefully evaluating the properties of available physical devices, you can select the one that best meets the needs of your application.

Code Example: Enumerating Physical Devices

C++

```cpp
// Create a Vulkan instance (details omitted for brevity)

VkInstance instance;


// Get the number of available physical devices

uint32_t deviceCount = 0;

vkEnumeratePhysicalDevices(instance, &deviceCount, nullptr);


// Allocate an array to store the physical device handles

std::vector<VkPhysicalDevice> devices(deviceCount);

vkEnumeratePhysicalDevices(instance, &deviceCount, devices.data());
```

```cpp
// Iterate over the devices and print their properties

for (const auto& device : devices) {

    VkPhysicalDeviceProperties deviceProperties;

    vkGetPhysicalDeviceProperties(device, &deviceProperties);

    std::cout << "Device Name: " << deviceProperties.deviceName << std::endl;

    // ... print other properties ...

}
```

This code snippet demonstrates how to enumerate the available physical devices and retrieve their properties. You can then use this information to select the most suitable device for your application.

By understanding the roles of the Vulkan instance and physical devices, you establish a solid foundation for interacting with the graphics hardware and building your Vulkan applications.

Logical Devices and Queues

After selecting a suitable physical device, the next step is to create a logical device. This logical device acts as an intermediary between your application and the physical GPU, providing a more manageable interface for submitting commands and managing resources.

Creating a Logical Device

Creating a logical device involves specifying several parameters that influence its behavior and capabilities:

- **Queues:** You need to specify which queues you want to create for this logical device. Queues are responsible for submitting work to the GPU, and different queues might be specialized for different types of tasks (graphics, compute, transfer).
- **Features:** You can enable optional features supported by the physical device, such as geometry shaders, tessellation, or specific texture compression formats.
- **Extensions:** You can enable optional extensions to access additional functionality not included in the core Vulkan API.

Queues: The Workhorses of Vulkan

Queues are fundamental to Vulkan's operation. They represent channels through which you submit commands to the GPU for execution. Each queue belongs to a queue family, and queue families are categorized by the types of operations they support. Common queue types include:

- **Graphics Queues:** Handle traditional graphics rendering commands, such as drawing triangles, rendering textures, and applying shaders.
- **Compute Queues:** Execute compute shaders, which are used for general-purpose parallel computation on the GPU.
- **Transfer Queues:** Specialized for transferring data between different memory locations, such as between the host memory and the device memory.

When creating a logical device, you specify which queues you need from each queue family. You might request multiple queues from the same family to enable parallel execution of different tasks.

Submitting Commands to Queues

Vulkan uses command buffers to record sequences of commands that are then submitted to queues for execution. These commands can include operations like:

- **Drawing Operations:** vkCmdDraw, vkCmdDrawIndexed
- **Compute Operations:** vkCmdDispatch
- **Memory Transfers:** vkCmdCopyBuffer, vkCmdCopyImage
- **State Changes:** vkCmdBindPipeline, vkCmdSetViewport

Once a command buffer is filled with commands, it can be submitted to a queue using the vkQueueSubmit function. The GPU then processes the commands asynchronously.

Synchronization and Fences

Vulkan provides mechanisms for synchronizing operations both within the GPU and between the CPU and GPU. This is crucial for ensuring that commands are executed in the correct order and that data dependencies are respected.

- **Semaphores:** Used to synchronize operations within the GPU, such as ensuring that a compute shader finishes execution before a graphics rendering operation starts.
- **Fences:** Used to synchronize operations between the CPU and GPU. They allow the CPU to wait for a specific command buffer to finish execution on the GPU.

Code Example: Creating a Logical Device and Retrieving Queues

C++

```cpp
// Select a physical device (details omitted for brevity)
VkPhysicalDevice physicalDevice;


// Get queue family properties
uint32_t queueFamilyCount = 0;
vkGetPhysicalDeviceQueueFamilyProperties(physicalDevice, &queueFamilyCount, nullptr);
std::vector<VkQueueFamilyProperties> queueFamilies(queueFamilyCount);
vkGetPhysicalDeviceQueueFamilyProperties(physicalDevice, &queueFamilyCount, queueFamilies.data());


// Find a suitable queue family (e.g., one that supports graphics operations)
uint32_t graphicsQueueFamilyIndex = 0;
for (uint32_t i = 0; i < queueFamilyCount; i++) {
```

```cpp
            if    (queueFamilies[i].queueFlags    &
VK_QUEUE_GRAPHICS_BIT) {

    graphicsQueueFamilyIndex = i;

    break;

  }

}


// Create a queue create info structure

float queuePriority = 1.0f;

VkDeviceQueueCreateInfo queueCreateInfo{};

queueCreateInfo.sType                              =
VK_STRUCTURE_TYPE_DEVICE_QUEUE_CREAT
E_INFO;

queueCreateInfo.queueFamilyIndex                  =
graphicsQueueFamilyIndex;

queueCreateInfo.queueCount = 1;

queueCreateInfo.pQueuePriorities = &queuePriority;


// Create the logical device

VkDeviceCreateInfo deviceCreateInfo{};
```

```
deviceCreateInfo.sType                        =
VK_STRUCTURE_TYPE_DEVICE_CREATE_INFO;

deviceCreateInfo.queueCreateInfoCount = 1;

deviceCreateInfo.pQueueCreateInfos            =
&queueCreateInfo;

// ... other device create info parameters ...


VkDevice device;

vkCreateDevice(physicalDevice,      &deviceCreateInfo,
nullptr, &device);


// Retrieve the graphics queue handle

VkQueue graphicsQueue;

vkGetDeviceQueue(device, graphicsQueueFamilyIndex,
0, &graphicsQueue);
```

This code snippet demonstrates how to create a logical device with a graphics queue and retrieve a handle to that queue. You can then use this queue to submit command buffers for graphics rendering.

By understanding the concepts of logical devices and queues, you gain the ability to interact with the GPU, submit commands, and manage resources effectively in your Vulkan applications.

Memory Management

Memory management is a critical aspect of Vulkan development. Unlike older APIs that often abstracted away memory details, Vulkan gives you explicit control over how memory is allocated, used, and managed. This control offers significant performance advantages but also requires a deeper understanding of Vulkan's memory model.

Types of Memory

Vulkan distinguishes between two main types of memory:

- **Host Memory:** This is the system memory accessible by the CPU. It's the memory you typically use for general-purpose programming.
- **Device Memory:** This is the memory residing on the graphics card itself. It's much faster for the GPU to access, making it ideal for storing resources that the GPU needs frequently, such as textures, vertex buffers, and uniform buffers.

Memory Heaps and Types

Each physical device has one or more memory heaps, which are large pools of memory with different characteristics. Within each heap, there are different memory types, each with specific properties:

- **Host Visible:** Indicates whether the CPU can directly access this memory type.
- **Host Coherent:** Determines whether changes made by the CPU are immediately visible to the GPU (and vice versa).
- **Host Cached:** Indicates whether the CPU caches this memory type, potentially improving CPU access performance.
- **Device Local:** Specifies whether this memory type is located on the device (GPU) itself, offering the fastest access for the GPU.

Memory Allocation

To allocate memory in Vulkan, you need to:

1. **Determine Memory Requirements:** Use functions like vkGetBufferMemoryRequirements or vkGetImageMemoryRequirements to determine the size and memory type requirements of your resource (buffer or image).
2. **Find a Suitable Memory Type:** Iterate through the memory types available in the physical device's memory heaps and find one that satisfies the requirements of your resource.

3. **Allocate Memory:** Use the vkAllocateMemory function to allocate a block of memory from the chosen memory type.
4. **Bind Memory:** Associate the allocated memory with your resource using functions like vkBindBufferMemory or vkBindImageMemory.

Memory Mapping

If you need to access device memory from the CPU (e.g., to upload data to a buffer), you can map it to host memory using the vkMapMemory function. This gives you a pointer to the device memory that you can use from the CPU. Remember to unmap the memory when you're finished using vkUnmapMemory.

Staging Buffers

For optimal performance, it's often best to avoid frequent direct access to device memory from the CPU. Instead, you can use staging buffers:

1. **Create a Staging Buffer:** Allocate a buffer in host-visible memory.
2. **Copy Data to Staging Buffer:** Copy your data from the CPU to the staging buffer.
3. **Transfer to Device Memory:** Use a transfer queue to copy the data from the staging buffer to the buffer in device local memory.

Memory Aliasing

Vulkan allows you to create multiple resources that share the same underlying memory allocation. This can be useful for situations where you have different views of the same data.

Sparse Memory

Vulkan supports sparse memory, which allows you to allocate and use large memory regions without having to commit all the physical memory upfront. This is particularly useful for managing very large textures or data sets.

Code Example: Allocating and Binding Buffer Memory

```cpp
C++

// Create a buffer (details omitted for brevity)

VkBuffer buffer;


// Get memory requirements for the buffer

VkMemoryRequirements memRequirements;

vkGetBufferMemoryRequirements(device,        buffer,
&memRequirements);
```

```cpp
// Find a suitable memory type

uint32_t            memoryTypeIndex            =
findMemoryType(physicalDevice,
memRequirements.memoryTypeBits,
VK_MEMORY_PROPERTY_HOST_VISIBLE_BIT    |
VK_MEMORY_PROPERTY_HOST_COHERENT_BI
T);


// Allocate memory

VkMemoryAllocateInfo allocInfo{};

allocInfo.sType                            =
VK_STRUCTURE_TYPE_MEMORY_ALLOCATE_IN
FO;

allocInfo.allocationSize = memRequirements.size;

allocInfo.memoryTypeIndex = memoryTypeIndex;


VkDeviceMemory bufferMemory;

vkAllocateMemory(device,       &allocInfo,       nullptr,
&bufferMemory);
```

```
// Bind the memory to the buffer

vkBindBufferMemory(device, buffer, bufferMemory, 0);
```

This code demonstrates how to allocate memory for a buffer and bind that memory to the buffer. The findMemoryType function (not shown here) would iterate through the available memory types to find one that matches the requirements.

By mastering Vulkan's memory management capabilities, you can optimize your applications for performance and efficiency, ensuring that your graphics resources are stored and accessed in the most effective way possible.

Swapchains and Surface Presentation

In Vulkan, the swapchain plays a crucial role in presenting rendered images to the user's display. It acts as a bridge between your rendering operations and the windowing system, managing a set of buffers that are swapped to create smooth animation and prevent tearing.

Creating a Swapchain

Creating a swapchain involves a series of steps:

1. **Surface Creation:** First, you need to create a Vulkan surface that represents the window or display where you want to present your images. This typically involves interacting with the windowing system API (e.g., GLFW, SDL).
2. **Querying Surface Capabilities:** Next, you query the surface capabilities to determine supported presentation modes, image formats, and other relevant properties. This ensures compatibility between your rendering setup and the display.
3. **Choosing Swapchain Parameters:** Based on the surface capabilities, you choose appropriate parameters for your swapchain, such as the number of images, image format, and presentation mode.
4. **Creating the Swapchain:** Finally, you use the vkCreateSwapchainKHR function to create the swapchain object itself.

Swapchain Images

The swapchain manages a set of images, typically two or three, that act as rendering targets. These images are swapped in a synchronized manner to present the rendered content to the display.

Presentation Modes

Vulkan offers different presentation modes that control how images are presented to the screen:

- **FIFO (First-In, First-Out):** The most common mode, it queues presented images in a FIFO queue, waiting for the next vertical blanking interval (V-sync) to display the next image. This prevents tearing but can introduce input lag.
- **Immediate:** Presents images immediately, potentially causing tearing but minimizing latency.
- **Mailbox:** A more advanced mode that allows you to submit images to a mailbox, with the most recent image being displayed at the next V-sync. This can reduce latency while still preventing tearing.

Acquiring and Presenting Images

To render a new frame, you need to acquire an image from the swapchain using the vkAcquireNextImageKHR function. This gives you an index to the next available image in the swapchain that you can use as a rendering target.

Once you've finished rendering to the image, you present it to the screen using the vkQueuePresentKHR function. This submits the image to the presentation queue, where it will be displayed at the appropriate time according to the chosen presentation mode.

Synchronization

Synchronization is essential when working with swapchains to ensure that you don't render to an image that is currently being presented or acquire an image that is still being rendered to. Semaphores and fences are used to coordinate these operations.

Handling Swapchain Recreation

The swapchain might need to be recreated in certain situations, such as when the window is resized or the display mode changes. You need to handle these events and recreate the swapchain with the new parameters.

Code Example: Basic Swapchain Creation

C++

```
// Create a Vulkan surface (details omitted for brevity)

VkSurfaceKHR surface;


// ... Query surface capabilities and choose swapchain parameters ...
```

```
VkSwapchainCreateInfoKHR createInfo{};

createInfo.sType                          =
VK_STRUCTURE_TYPE_SWAPCHAIN_CREATE_IN
FO_KHR;

createInfo.surface = surface;

// ... other swapchain parameters ...


VkSwapchainKHR swapchain;

vkCreateSwapchainKHR(device,  &createInfo,  nullptr,
&swapchain);
```

This code snippet demonstrates the basic structure of creating a swapchain. You would need to fill in the details based on the surface capabilities and your desired swapchain parameters.

By understanding the concepts of swapchains and surface presentation, you gain the ability to display your rendered images on the screen, creating smooth animation and interactive graphics applications.

A First Vulkan Triangle: Bringing it All Together

It's time to put all the pieces together and render our first Vulkan triangle! This classic exercise will solidify your understanding of the fundamental concepts we've covered so far and provide a practical starting point for your Vulkan applications.

Steps to Render a Triangle

1. **Instance and Device Creation:** Begin by creating a Vulkan instance and selecting a suitable physical device. Then, create a logical device with the necessary queues (graphics queue in this case).

2. **Swapchain Setup:** Create a swapchain to manage the presentation of images to the screen. Obtain handles to the swapchain images, which will be used as rendering targets.

3. **Render Pass:** Define a render pass that specifies how the rendering operations will be performed. This includes aspects like attachments (color, depth), clear values, and dependencies between subpasses.

4. **Pipeline:** Create a graphics pipeline that defines the sequence of operations for processing vertices and fragments. This involves creating shader modules, specifying vertex input descriptions,

and configuring rasterization and other pipeline stages.

5. **Command Buffers:** Allocate and record command buffers that contain the actual drawing commands. These commands include binding the pipeline, setting up vertex and index buffers, and issuing the draw call.

6. **Synchronization:** Use semaphores and fences to synchronize the acquisition and presentation of swapchain images with the rendering process.

7. **Main Loop:** In the main loop, acquire an image from the swapchain, submit the command buffer to the graphics queue, and then present the rendered image to the screen.

Simplified Code Example

```cpp
C++

// ... Instance, device, and swapchain creation ...


// Create render pass, pipeline, and command buffers ...


while (!glfwWindowShouldClose(window)) {

  glfwPollEvents();
```

```cpp
uint32_t imageIndex;

vkAcquireNextImageKHR(device, swapchain,
UINT64_MAX, imageAvailableSemaphore,
VK_NULL_HANDLE, &imageIndex);


VkSubmitInfo submitInfo{};

submitInfo.sType =
VK_STRUCTURE_TYPE_SUBMIT_INFO;

submitInfo.waitSemaphoreCount = 1;

submitInfo.pWaitSemaphores =
&imageAvailableSemaphore;

VkPipelineStageFlags waitStages[] =
{VK_PIPELINE_STAGE_COLOR_ATTACHMENT_O
UTPUT_BIT};

submitInfo.pWaitDstStageMask = waitStages;

submitInfo.commandBufferCount = 1;

submitInfo.pCommandBuffers =
&commandBuffers[imageIndex];

submitInfo.signalSemaphoreCount = 1;
```

```cpp
        submitInfo.pSignalSemaphores    =
&renderFinishedSemaphore;


    vkQueueSubmit(graphicsQueue, 1, &submitInfo,
VK_NULL_HANDLE);


    VkPresentInfoKHR presentInfo{};

                    presentInfo.sType       =
VK_STRUCTURE_TYPE_PRESENT_INFO_KHR;

    presentInfo.waitSemaphoreCount = 1;

                presentInfo.pWaitSemaphores   =
&renderFinishedSemaphore;

    presentInfo.swapchainCount = 1;

    presentInfo.pSwapchains = &swapchain;

    presentInfo.pImageIndices = &imageIndex;


    vkQueuePresentKHR(presentQueue, &presentInfo);
}


// ... Cleanup and resource destruction ...
```

Explanation

This simplified code demonstrates the core loop of a Vulkan application. It acquires a swapchain image, submits a command buffer that contains the rendering commands, and then presents the rendered image. The semaphores ensure proper synchronization between these operations.

Challenges and Considerations

Rendering a simple triangle in Vulkan might seem like a lot of code compared to older APIs. This is because Vulkan gives you more control and requires you to handle many details explicitly. However, this control translates to greater performance and flexibility in the long run.

As you progress with Vulkan development, you'll encounter challenges like shader compilation, pipeline creation, and memory management. Don't be discouraged! These challenges are opportunities to deepen your understanding of Vulkan and its capabilities.

By successfully rendering your first Vulkan triangle, you've taken a significant step in your Vulkan development journey. You now have a solid foundation to build upon as you explore more advanced rendering techniques and create complex graphics applications.

Chapter 3: Shaders and the Graphics Pipeline

The Rendering Pipeline in Detail

The rendering pipeline is the heart of any graphics system, and Vulkan's implementation offers a remarkable level of flexibility and control. This section provides a detailed examination of the Vulkan rendering pipeline, highlighting its key stages and the flow of data from vertices to pixels.

1. Input Assembly:

The journey begins with raw vertex data, which describes the geometric shapes of your 3D models. The input assembly stage gathers this data from vertex buffers and arranges it into primitives, such as points, lines, or triangles. You have control over the input format, allowing you to specify how vertex attributes (position, color, normals, etc.) are organized in memory.

2. Vertex Shading:

Vertex shaders are small programs that operate on individual vertices. They are responsible for transforming vertices from model space to screen space, applying skinning animations, and performing other per-vertex calculations. Each vertex undergoes transformation, and the output is a clip-space coordinate.

3. Tessellation (Optional):

Tessellation is an optional stage that can subdivide primitives into smaller, more detailed primitives. This allows for dynamic level-of-detail rendering and the creation of smooth curved surfaces from simpler base shapes. Tessellation control and evaluation shaders work in tandem to control the subdivision process and generate new vertices.

4. Geometry Shading (Optional):

Geometry shaders operate on entire primitives, allowing you to modify or generate new primitives on the fly. This stage can be used for effects like fur rendering, shadow volume extrusion, and particle system generation.

5. Rasterization:

The rasterization stage converts transformed primitives into fragments. It determines which pixels on the screen are covered by each primitive and interpolates vertex attributes across the surface of the primitive. This stage also performs clipping, discarding any parts of primitives that fall outside the viewing frustum.

6. Fragment Shading:

Fragment shaders are programs that operate on individual fragments. They are responsible for determining the final color of each pixel, taking into account lighting, textures, and other material properties. Fragment shaders can perform complex calculations and utilize various techniques to achieve a wide range of visual effects.

7. Color Blending:

The color blending stage combines the output of the fragment shader with the existing color in the framebuffer. This allows for effects like transparency, alpha blending, and additive blending. You have control over the blending equation and factors to achieve different blending modes.

8. Output Merging:

The final stage of the pipeline handles operations like depth testing, stencil testing, and multisampling. Depth testing ensures that objects closer to the viewer occlude objects further away. Stencil testing allows for masking and selective rendering based on stencil values. Multisampling improves image quality by reducing aliasing artifacts.

Vulkan's Pipeline State Object

In Vulkan, the entire rendering pipeline is encapsulated in a pipeline state object (PSO). This object holds all the configuration parameters for each stage of the pipeline, including shader modules, vertex input descriptions, rasterization state, and blending state. Creating a PSO upfront allows the driver to perform optimizations and reduces the overhead of switching between different pipeline states.

Flexibility and Control

Vulkan's rendering pipeline provides exceptional flexibility and control. You can customize almost every aspect of the pipeline, from vertex input to output merging. This allows you to tailor the rendering process to your specific needs and achieve a wide range of visual effects.

Example: A Simple Pipeline

```cpp
C++

// ... Shader module creation ...


VkPipelineShaderStageCreateInfo
vertShaderStageInfo{};
```

```
vertShaderStageInfo.sType                =
VK_STRUCTURE_TYPE_PIPELINE_SHADER_STA
GE_CREATE_INFO;

vertShaderStageInfo.stage                =
VK_SHADER_STAGE_VERTEX_BIT;

vertShaderStageInfo.module = vertShaderModule;

vertShaderStageInfo.pName = "main";


VkPipelineShaderStageCreateInfo
fragShaderStageInfo{};

fragShaderStageInfo.sType                =
VK_STRUCTURE_TYPE_PIPELINE_SHADER_STA
GE_CREATE_INFO;

fragShaderStageInfo.stage                =
VK_SHADER_STAGE_FRAGMENT_BIT;

fragShaderStageInfo.module = fragShaderModule;

fragShaderStageInfo.pName = "main";


VkPipelineShaderStageCreateInfo    shaderStages[]    =
{vertShaderStageInfo, fragShaderStageInfo};
```

```
// ... Vertex input state, input assembly state, viewport
state, etc. ...


VkGraphicsPipelineCreateInfo pipelineInfo{};

pipelineInfo.sType                              =
VK_STRUCTURE_TYPE_GRAPHICS_PIPELINE_CR
EATE_INFO;

pipelineInfo.stageCount = 2;

pipelineInfo.pStages = shaderStages;

// ... other pipeline state information ...


VkPipeline graphicsPipeline;

vkCreateGraphicsPipelines(device,
VK_NULL_HANDLE,    1,    &pipelineInfo,    nullptr,
&graphicsPipeline);
```

This code snippet illustrates the creation of a basic
graphics pipeline with a vertex shader and a fragment
shader. You would need to fill in the other pipeline state
information based on your specific rendering
requirements.

By understanding the Vulkan rendering pipeline in detail, you can harness its power to create stunning visuals and achieve optimal performance in your graphics applications.

Vertex Shaders: Processing Geometry

Vertex shaders are the workhorses of 3D graphics, responsible for manipulating the geometry of your models before they are rendered to the screen. In Vulkan, you write vertex shaders in GLSL (OpenGL Shading Language) and compile them into SPIR-V, a portable intermediate representation that can be understood by the Vulkan driver.

The Role of a Vertex Shader

The primary function of a vertex shader is to process individual vertices and transform them from model space to clip space. This transformation involves several steps:

1. **Model Transformation:** Transforms vertices from their local coordinate system (model space) to the world coordinate system. This accounts for the position, rotation, and scale of the model within the scene.
2. **View Transformation:** Transforms vertices from world space to view space, which is the

coordinate system relative to the camera's position and orientation.

3. **Projection Transformation:** Transforms vertices from view space to clip space, which is a normalized coordinate system that defines the visible region of the scene. This step accounts for the perspective projection or orthographic projection used by the camera.

Input and Output

A vertex shader receives input data in the form of vertex attributes. These attributes can include:

- **Position:** The 3D coordinates of the vertex.
- **Color:** The color of the vertex.
- **Normal:** A vector that defines the surface orientation at the vertex.
- **Texture Coordinates:** Coordinates that map the vertex to a point on a texture.

The output of a vertex shader is a clip-space position, which is a 4D vector (gl_Position in GLSL). This position is used by subsequent stages of the pipeline for clipping, perspective division, and viewport transformation.

Beyond Basic Transformations

Vertex shaders can perform much more than just basic transformations. They can also:

- **Calculate lighting:** Compute lighting contributions at each vertex based on light sources and material properties.
- **Apply skinning:** Deform the mesh based on skeletal animation data.
- **Generate procedural geometry:** Create or modify geometry dynamically within the shader.
- **Pass data to fragment shaders:** Calculate and output values that will be interpolated and used by the fragment shader.

Example: A Simple Vertex Shader

OpenGL Shading Language

```
#version 450


layout(location = 0) in vec3 inPosition;

layout(location = 1) in vec3 inColor;


layout(location = 0) out vec3 fragColor;
```

```
void main() {

  gl_Position = vec4(inPosition, 1.0);

  fragColor = inColor;

}
```

This simple vertex shader takes a vertex position and color as input, transforms the position to clip space, and passes the color to the fragment shader.

Compiling Shaders

To use a vertex shader in your Vulkan application, you need to compile it into SPIR-V using the glslangValidator tool from the Vulkan SDK. This tool converts your GLSL code into a binary format that can be loaded and used by the Vulkan driver.

Flexibility and Power

Vertex shaders provide immense flexibility and power for manipulating geometry and creating a wide range of visual effects. By understanding how to write and utilize vertex shaders, you can unlock the full potential of Vulkan's rendering pipeline.

Fragment Shaders: Coloring Pixels

Fragment shaders are the artists of the rendering pipeline, responsible for determining the final color of each pixel that appears on the screen. They operate on individual fragments, which are generated by the rasterization stage, and take into account various factors such as lighting, textures, and material properties to produce the desired visual output.

The Role of a Fragment Shader

The primary function of a fragment shader is to calculate the color and other properties of each pixel. This involves:

1. **Receiving Input:** Fragment shaders receive input data in the form of interpolated vertex attributes. These attributes are passed from the vertex shader and smoothly vary across the surface of the primitive.
2. **Accessing Textures:** Fragment shaders can sample textures to retrieve color information, normal maps, or other data that influences the pixel's appearance.
3. **Calculating Lighting:** Fragment shaders can implement lighting models to calculate the interaction of light with the surface, taking into

account light sources, surface normals, and material properties.

4. **Applying Effects:** Fragment shaders can apply a wide range of visual effects, such as shadows, reflections, and post-processing filters.

5. **Outputting Color:** The final output of a fragment shader is a color value (fragColor in GLSL) that is written to the framebuffer.

Input and Output

Fragment shaders receive input data in the form of interpolated vertex attributes. These attributes are passed from the vertex shader and smoothly vary across the surface of the primitive. Common input attributes include:

- **Interpolated Position:** The 3D position of the fragment in world space or screen space.
- **Interpolated Color:** The color of the fragment, interpolated from the vertex colors.
- **Interpolated Normal:** The surface normal at the fragment, interpolated from the vertex normals.
- **Interpolated Texture Coordinates:** The texture coordinates at the fragment, interpolated from the vertex texture coordinates.

The output of a fragment shader is typically a color value (fragColor in GLSL) that is written to the framebuffer.

However, fragment shaders can also output other values, such as depth values or stencil values, to control specific rendering effects.

Example: A Simple Fragment Shader

OpenGL Shading Language

```
#version 450


layout(location = 0) in vec3 fragColor;


layout(location = 0) out vec4 outColor;


void main() {
  outColor = vec4(fragColor, 1.0);
}
```

This simple fragment shader receives a color value from the vertex shader and outputs it directly to the framebuffer.

Advanced Techniques

Fragment shaders can implement a wide range of advanced rendering techniques, such as:

- **Deferred Shading:** A technique that decouples lighting calculations from surface shading, allowing for more efficient rendering of complex scenes.
- **Shadow Mapping:** A technique for generating shadows by comparing the depth of a fragment to a depth map generated from the light's perspective.
- **Normal Mapping:** A technique for adding surface detail by perturbing the surface normal based on a normal map texture.
- **Post-Processing Effects:** Effects applied to the rendered image after the main rendering pass, such as bloom, blur, and color grading.

Flexibility and Creativity

Fragment shaders provide immense flexibility and creative potential for achieving a wide range of visual effects. By mastering the art of fragment shader programming, you can bring your 3D scenes to life with stunning realism and artistic expression.

Shader Modules and Pipeline Creation

In Vulkan, shaders are not directly used in their raw source code form. Instead, they are compiled into SPIR-V (Standard Portable Intermediate Representation - V) and then encapsulated within shader modules. These modules serve as containers for the compiled shader code and are used during the creation of graphics pipelines.

Creating Shader Modules

To create a shader module, you need to load the compiled SPIR-V code and pass it to the vkCreateShaderModule function. This function takes the shader code as input and returns a handle to the newly created shader module.

The Graphics Pipeline

The graphics pipeline is a sequence of stages that define how graphics data is processed and rendered. It encompasses various operations, from vertex processing and rasterization to fragment shading and output merging. In Vulkan, you create a graphics pipeline object that encapsulates all the configuration parameters for these stages.

Pipeline Creation

Creating a graphics pipeline involves specifying a wide range of parameters, including:

- **Shader Stages:** You need to specify the shader modules for each stage of the pipeline, such as the vertex shader and fragment shader.
- **Vertex Input:** You describe the format of the vertex data that will be input to the pipeline, including the attributes and their locations.
- **Input Assembly:** You specify the type of primitives that will be assembled from the vertex data, such as points, lines, or triangles.
- **Viewport and Scissor:** You define the viewport and scissor rectangles that control the portion of the output image that will be rendered to.
- **Rasterization:** You configure rasterization settings, such as polygon mode, culling mode, and depth bias.
- **Multisampling:** You enable or disable multisampling, which is a technique for improving image quality by reducing aliasing.
- **Depth and Stencil Testing:** You configure depth and stencil testing, which control how fragments are discarded or blended based on their depth and stencil values.
- **Color Blending:** You specify how the output of the fragment shader is blended with the existing color in the framebuffer.

Pipeline State Object (PSO)

The graphics pipeline is represented by a pipeline state object (PSO). This object holds all the configuration parameters for the pipeline and is used during rendering to instruct the GPU how to process graphics data. Creating a PSO upfront allows the driver to perform optimizations and reduces the overhead of switching between different pipeline states.

Code Example: Creating a Shader Module and Graphics Pipeline

```
C++

// Load SPIR-V code from file

std::vector<char>        vertShaderCode      =
readFile("vert.spv");

std::vector<char>        fragShaderCode      =
readFile("frag.spv");


// Create shader modules

VkShaderModule        vertShaderModule      =
createShaderModule(device, vertShaderCode);

VkShaderModule        fragShaderModule      =
createShaderModule(device, fragShaderCode);
```

```
// ... Pipeline creation (refer to previous example) ...


// Destroy shader modules

vkDestroyShaderModule(device,          fragShaderModule,
nullptr);

vkDestroyShaderModule(device,          vertShaderModule,
nullptr);
```

This code snippet demonstrates how to create shader modules from SPIR-V code and use them in the creation of a graphics pipeline.

Benefits of Pipeline Creation

Creating graphics pipelines in Vulkan offers several benefits:

- **Performance:** Creating PSOs upfront allows the driver to perform optimizations and reduces runtime overhead.
- **Flexibility:** You have fine-grained control over every stage of the pipeline, allowing you to tailor the rendering process to your specific needs.

- **Maintainability:** Encapsulating pipeline state in a single object improves code organization and makes it easier to manage different rendering configurations.

By understanding the process of shader module creation and pipeline creation, you gain a deeper understanding of how Vulkan's rendering pipeline works and how to configure it to achieve the desired visual results.

Debugging and Profiling Your Shaders

As you develop more complex shaders, you're bound to encounter errors or performance bottlenecks. Fortunately, Vulkan provides tools and techniques for debugging and profiling your shaders, helping you identify and resolve issues effectively.

Validation Layers

Vulkan's validation layers are invaluable for catching errors during development. They act as a safety net, monitoring your API usage and reporting any violations of the Vulkan specification. Enable validation layers during development to receive warnings and error messages that can help you identify issues such as:

- **Invalid API usage:** Passing incorrect parameters to Vulkan functions, using objects that have been destroyed, or violating resource lifecycle rules.

- **Shader compilation errors:** Errors in your shader code that prevent it from compiling correctly.
- **Pipeline state inconsistencies:** Mismatches between shader stages or incorrect pipeline state configurations.

Debugging with RenderDoc

RenderDoc is a powerful graphics debugger that allows you to capture and inspect frames from your Vulkan application. It provides a wealth of information about the rendering process, including:

- **Shader debugging:** Step through your shader code line by line, inspect variables, and identify logic errors.
- **Pipeline state inspection:** Examine the configuration of your graphics pipeline, including shader modules, vertex input, and rasterization state.
- **Resource inspection:** View the contents of textures, buffers, and other resources used in your rendering.
- **Performance analysis:** Identify performance bottlenecks by examining draw calls, pipeline state changes, and memory access patterns.

Profiling with Vulkan Profiling Layers

The Vulkan SDK includes profiling layers that can collect detailed performance data about your application. These layers can help you identify:

- **CPU bottlenecks:** Functions or code sections that are taking excessive time on the CPU.
- **GPU bottlenecks:** Shader stages or rendering operations that are limiting the overall performance.
- **Memory transfer overhead:** Inefficient data transfers between the CPU and GPU.

Optimizing Shader Performance

Once you've identified performance bottlenecks in your shaders, you can apply various optimization techniques to improve their efficiency:

- **Reduce unnecessary calculations:** Avoid redundant calculations or complex operations that are not essential for the desired visual result.
- **Optimize memory access:** Use constant memory for frequently accessed data, and minimize memory fetches by utilizing local variables and registers effectively.
- **Unroll loops:** Unroll small loops to reduce loop overhead, but be mindful of the potential increase in code size.

- **Use built-in functions:** Leverage Vulkan's built-in functions for common operations, as they are often optimized for the underlying hardware.
- **Avoid branching:** Branching can disrupt the parallel execution of shaders, so try to minimize conditional statements or use techniques like predication to avoid them.

Best Practices

- **Enable validation layers during development:** Catch errors early and ensure your code adheres to the Vulkan specification.
- **Use a graphics debugger like RenderDoc:** Inspect frames, debug shaders, and analyze pipeline state.
- **Profile your application with Vulkan profiling layers:** Identify performance bottlenecks and optimize your shaders accordingly.
- **Write clean and efficient shader code:** Follow best practices for shader optimization to maximize performance.

By utilizing these debugging and profiling techniques, you can ensure that your shaders are not only correct but also performant, contributing to the overall efficiency and visual quality of your Vulkan applications.

Chapter 4: Drawing and Transformations

Vertex Buffers and Input Descriptions

In the realm of 3D graphics, vertices are the fundamental building blocks of our virtual worlds. They define the shape and structure of objects, forming the foundation upon which textures, lighting, and other visual effects are applied. To efficiently process and render these vertices, Vulkan employs vertex buffers and input descriptions, providing a streamlined mechanism for feeding vertex data to the graphics pipeline.

Vertex Buffers: Organized Vertex Data

A vertex buffer is essentially a contiguous block of memory that stores vertex data in an organized manner. This data typically includes attributes such as:

- **Position:** The 3D coordinates of the vertex in model space.
- **Color:** The color associated with the vertex.
- **Normal:** A vector that defines the surface orientation at the vertex, used for lighting calculations.
- **Texture Coordinates:** Coordinates that map the vertex to a point on a texture image.

- **Tangent and Bitangent:** Vectors that define the tangent space at the vertex, used for advanced lighting and normal mapping techniques.

By storing vertex data in a structured format within a buffer, Vulkan can efficiently access and process this information during rendering.

Creating Vertex Buffers

Creating a vertex buffer in Vulkan involves several steps:

1. **Memory Allocation:** Allocate a block of memory from the device memory that is suitable for storing vertex data. This typically involves choosing a memory type that is both device-local (for optimal GPU access) and host-visible (for initial data population).
2. **Buffer Creation:** Create a Vulkan buffer object that represents the vertex buffer. Specify the size of the buffer and its intended usage (e.g., vertex buffer, transfer destination).
3. **Data Population:** Populate the buffer with your vertex data. This can be done by mapping the buffer memory to host memory and copying the data directly, or by using staging buffers for more efficient data transfer.

4. **Binding:** Bind the vertex buffer to the graphics pipeline so that the vertex shader can access the data during rendering.

Input Descriptions: Guiding the Pipeline

While vertex buffers hold the raw vertex data, input descriptions provide the necessary context for the graphics pipeline to interpret this data correctly. An input description specifies:

- **Binding:** Which vertex buffer the attribute data comes from.
- **Location:** The location index of the attribute within the vertex shader.
- **Format:** The data type and format of the attribute (e.g., float3, vec2, int).
- **Offset:** The byte offset within the vertex data structure where the attribute starts.

By providing this information, the input description guides the pipeline in fetching the correct attribute data from the vertex buffer and feeding it to the vertex shader.

Vertex Input State

The vertex input state is a structure that encapsulates the input descriptions for all the attributes used by the vertex shader. This state is part of the graphics pipeline creation process and informs the pipeline about the structure and layout of the vertex data.

Code Example: Creating a Vertex Buffer and Input Description

C++

```
// ... Memory allocation and buffer creation ...


// Define vertex input binding and attribute descriptions
VkVertexInputBindingDescription bindingDescription{};

bindingDescription.binding = 0;

bindingDescription.stride = sizeof(Vertex);

bindingDescription.inputRate =
VK_VERTEX_INPUT_RATE_VERTEX;


std::array<VkVertexInputAttributeDescription,      2>
attributeDescriptions{};

attributeDescriptions[0].binding = 0;

attributeDescriptions[0].location = 0;
```

```
attributeDescriptions[0].format                    =
VK_FORMAT_R32G32B32_SFLOAT;

attributeDescriptions[0].offset = offsetof(Vertex, pos);


attributeDescriptions[1].binding = 0;

attributeDescriptions[1].location = 1;

attributeDescriptions[1].format                    =
VK_FORMAT_R32G32B32_SFLOAT;

attributeDescriptions[1].offset = offsetof(Vertex, color);


// Create pipeline vertex input state create info

VkPipelineVertexInputStateCreateInfo
vertexInputInfo{};

vertexInputInfo.sType                              =
VK_STRUCTURE_TYPE_PIPELINE_VERTEX_INPU
T_STATE_CREATE_INFO;

vertexInputInfo.vertexBindingDescriptionCount = 1;

vertexInputInfo.pVertexBindingDescriptions         =
&bindingDescription;

vertexInputInfo.vertexAttributeDescriptionCount    =
static_cast<uint32_t>(attributeDescriptions.size());
```

```
vertexInputInfo.pVertexAttributeDescriptions          =
attributeDescriptions.data();


// ... Use vertexInputInfo in pipeline creation ...
```

This code snippet demonstrates how to create a vertex buffer and define the input descriptions for the vertex attributes. The bindingDescription specifies the layout of the vertex data within the buffer, while the attributeDescriptions define the individual attributes and their formats.

By understanding the concepts of vertex buffers and input descriptions, you gain a crucial understanding of how vertex data is managed and processed in Vulkan, enabling you to efficiently render complex 3D scenes.

Index Buffers: Efficient Rendering

As you work with more complex 3D models, you'll often encounter situations where vertices are shared between multiple triangles. Storing these shared vertices repeatedly in your vertex buffer can lead to redundant data and increased memory usage. This is where index buffers come into play, offering a clever solution for optimizing vertex data and improving rendering efficiency.

The Purpose of Index Buffers

An index buffer is a separate buffer that stores indices, which are integer values that reference vertices in your vertex buffer. Instead of storing duplicate vertices, you store each unique vertex only once in the vertex buffer and then use the index buffer to define the order in which these vertices should be connected to form triangles.

Benefits of Using Index Buffers

- **Reduced Memory Usage:** By eliminating duplicate vertices, index buffers significantly reduce the amount of memory required to store your 3D models. This is especially beneficial for complex models with many shared vertices.
- **Improved Rendering Performance:** With less vertex data to process, the graphics pipeline can render your models more efficiently. This can lead to higher frame rates and smoother animation.
- **Simplified Mesh Construction:** Index buffers make it easier to construct complex meshes with shared vertices, as you only need to define each unique vertex once.

Creating and Using Index Buffers

Creating an index buffer follows a similar process to creating a vertex buffer:

1. **Memory Allocation:** Allocate a block of device memory suitable for storing index data.
2. **Buffer Creation:** Create a Vulkan buffer object to represent the index buffer.
3. **Data Population:** Populate the buffer with the indices that define the connectivity of your vertices.
4. **Binding:** Bind the index buffer to the graphics pipeline before issuing draw calls.

When issuing a draw call with an index buffer, you specify the number of indices to use and the offset within the index buffer where the drawing should start. The graphics pipeline then uses these indices to fetch the corresponding vertices from the vertex buffer and assemble the triangles.

Example: Rendering a Cube with an Index Buffer

Consider a cube, which has 8 vertices but 36 indices (6 faces * 2 triangles per face * 3 vertices per triangle). Using an index buffer, you store the 8 unique vertices in the vertex buffer and the 36 indices in the index buffer. This significantly reduces the amount of data that needs to be processed compared to storing all 36 vertices explicitly.

Code Example: Drawing with an Index Buffer

C++

```
// ... Create and populate index buffer ...


// Bind the index buffer

vkCmdBindIndexBuffer(commandBuffer, indexBuffer,
0, VK_INDEX_TYPE_UINT32);


// Draw indexed

vkCmdDrawIndexed(commandBuffer,
static_cast<uint32_t>(indices.size()), 1, 0, 0, 0);
```

This code snippet demonstrates how to bind an index buffer and issue a draw call that uses the index buffer to render the geometry.

Choosing the Right Index Type

Vulkan supports different index types, such as VK_INDEX_TYPE_UINT16 and VK_INDEX_TYPE_UINT32. Choose the appropriate type based on the number of vertices in your model. For smaller models, UINT16 might suffice, while larger models might require UINT32 to address all the vertices.

By utilizing index buffers effectively, you can optimize your Vulkan applications for both memory usage and rendering performance, enabling you to create more complex and detailed 3D scenes without sacrificing efficiency.

Uniform Buffers: Passing Data to Shaders

While vertex buffers provide the geometric foundation of your 3D models, and index buffers optimize their rendering, uniform buffers offer a powerful mechanism for dynamically supplying data to your shaders. They act as a bridge between your application's CPU-side logic and the GPU, allowing you to efficiently pass parameters that influence rendering behavior.

What are Uniform Buffers?

Uniform buffers are blocks of memory that store data that remains constant for multiple vertices or fragments within a draw call. This data can include:

- **Transformation matrices:** Model, view, and projection matrices that define the position, orientation, and scale of objects in the scene.

- **Lighting parameters:** Light positions, colors, and intensities that influence how objects are illuminated.
- **Material properties:** Color, reflectivity, and other characteristics that define the appearance of surfaces.
- **Time:** A continuously updated value that can be used for animations or time-based effects.
- **Custom parameters:** Any application-specific data that your shaders require.

By storing this data in uniform buffers, you avoid redundant transfers of the same data for each vertex or fragment, significantly improving rendering efficiency.

Creating and Updating Uniform Buffers

Creating a uniform buffer follows a similar process to creating vertex and index buffers:

1. **Memory Allocation:** Allocate a block of device memory that is suitable for storing the uniform data. This memory should be host-visible and coherent to allow for easy updates from the CPU.
2. **Buffer Creation:** Create a Vulkan buffer object to represent the uniform buffer.
3. **Data Population:** Initialize the buffer with the initial values of your uniform data.

4. **Updating Data:** When your uniform data needs to change, map the buffer memory to host memory, update the values, and then unmap the memory.

Descriptor Sets and Bindings

To make uniform buffers accessible to your shaders, you need to use descriptor sets and bindings.

*   **Descriptor Sets:** Act as containers for resources that your shaders need to access, including uniform buffers, textures, and samplers.
*   **Bindings:** Associate a specific resource within a descriptor set with a corresponding variable in your shader code.

You create descriptor sets and bindings during pipeline creation, specifying the types of resources that your shaders expect and their binding points.

Updating and Binding Descriptor Sets

Before rendering, you need to update the descriptor sets with the actual handles to your uniform buffers (and other resources). Then, you bind the descriptor set to the graphics pipeline, making the uniform data available to your shaders.

Code Example: Using a Uniform Buffer

C++

```cpp
// ... Create uniform buffer ...


// Define descriptor set layout and binding
VkDescriptorSetLayoutBinding uboLayoutBinding{};
uboLayoutBinding.binding = 0;
uboLayoutBinding.descriptorType                =
VK_DESCRIPTOR_TYPE_UNIFORM_BUFFER;
uboLayoutBinding.descriptorCount = 1;
uboLayoutBinding.stageFlags                =
VK_SHADER_STAGE_VERTEX_BIT;


// ... Create descriptor set layout, pipeline layout, and
descriptor pool ...


// Update descriptor set with uniform buffer handle
VkDescriptorBufferInfo bufferInfo{};
bufferInfo.buffer = uniformBuffer;
bufferInfo.offset = 0;
```

```cpp
bufferInfo.range = sizeof(UniformBufferObject);


VkWriteDescriptorSet descriptorWrite{};

descriptorWrite.sType                          =
VK_STRUCTURE_TYPE_WRITE_DESCRIPTOR_SE
T;

descriptorWrite.dstSet = descriptorSet;

descriptorWrite.dstBinding = 0;

descriptorWrite.dstArrayElement = 0;

descriptorWrite.descriptorType                 =
VK_DESCRIPTOR_TYPE_UNIFORM_BUFFER;

descriptorWrite.descriptorCount = 1;

descriptorWrite.pBufferInfo = &bufferInfo;


vkUpdateDescriptorSets(device, 1, &descriptorWrite, 0,
nullptr);


// Bind descriptor set
```

```
vkCmdBindDescriptorSets(commandBuffer,
VK_PIPELINE_BIND_POINT_GRAPHICS,
pipelineLayout, 0, 1, &descriptorSet, 0, nullptr);
```

This code snippet illustrates how to create and update a uniform buffer and make it accessible to your shaders through descriptor sets and bindings.

Efficiency and Flexibility

Uniform buffers provide an efficient and flexible way to pass data to your shaders, allowing you to dynamically control rendering behavior and create a wide range of visual effects. By mastering the use of uniform buffers, you can significantly enhance the expressiveness and dynamism of your Vulkan applications.

Transformations: Scaling, Rotating, and Translating

Transformations are fundamental to 3D graphics, allowing you to position, orient, and scale objects within your virtual world. In Vulkan, you typically handle transformations using matrices, which are mathematical constructs that efficiently represent these operations.

Types of Transformations

The three primary types of transformations are:

- **Scaling:** Changes the size of an object, making it larger or smaller along different axes.
- **Rotation:** Orients an object around a specific axis, changing its direction.
- **Translation:** Moves an object from one position to another in 3D space.

Transformation Matrices

Each transformation can be represented by a 4x4 matrix. These matrices are applied to the vertices of your 3D models to achieve the desired transformation effect.

- **Scaling Matrix:**

[sx 0 0 0]

[0 sy 0 0]

[0 0 sz 0]

[0 0 0 1]

where sx, sy, and sz are the scaling factors along the x, y, and z axes, respectively.

- **Rotation Matrix (around z-axis):**

[cos(θ) -sin(θ) 0 0]

[sin(θ) cos(θ) 0 0]

[0   0   1 0]

[0   0   0 1]

where θ is the angle of rotation. Similar matrices exist for rotations around the x and y axes.

- **Translation Matrix:**

[1 0 0 tx]

[0 1 0 ty]

[0 0 1 tz]

[0 0 0 1]

where tx, ty, and tz are the translation amounts along the x, y, and z axes, respectively.

Combining Transformations

You can combine multiple transformations by multiplying their matrices together. The order of multiplication matters, as it affects the final result. For example, rotating and then translating an object produces a different outcome than translating and then rotating it.

Transformations in Shaders

In Vulkan, you typically apply transformations within your vertex shader. You pass the transformation matrices as uniform variables to the shader and then multiply them with the vertex positions to achieve the desired transformation.

Example: Transforming a Vertex

OpenGL Shading Language

```
#version 450


layout(location = 0) in vec3 inPosition;


layout(binding = 0) uniform UniformBufferObject {
    mat4 model;
    mat4 view;
```

```
    mat4 proj;

} ubo;


void main() {

    gl_Position = ubo.proj * ubo.view * ubo.model *
vec4(inPosition, 1.0);

}
```

In this example, the vertex shader receives three
matrices: model, view, and proj. It multiplies these
matrices with the vertex position (inPosition) to
transform the vertex from model space to clip space.

glm Library

The glm (OpenGL Mathematics) library is a popular
choice for handling matrix operations in C++. It provides
functions for creating, manipulating, and multiplying
matrices, making it easier to work with transformations
in your Vulkan applications.

Transformations in Action

Transformations are essential for creating dynamic and
interactive 3D scenes. By understanding how to use

matrices to scale, rotate, and translate objects, you can bring your virtual worlds to life with movement, animation, and intricate spatial relationships.

Coordinate Systems and Projections

In 3D graphics, we work with various coordinate systems to represent the positions and orientations of objects in our virtual world. Understanding these coordinate systems and how they relate to each other is crucial for correctly transforming and rendering 3D scenes.

Common Coordinate Systems

- **Model Space:** The local coordinate system of a 3D model. Vertices are defined relative to the model's origin.
- **World Space:** The global coordinate system of the scene. Objects are positioned and oriented within the world.
- **View Space:** The coordinate system relative to the camera's position and orientation. Objects are transformed as if the camera is at the origin.
- **Clip Space:** A normalized coordinate system that defines the visible region of the scene. Objects outside this space are clipped.

- **Screen Space:** The 2D coordinate system of the screen or window where the final image is rendered.

Transformations Between Coordinate Systems

Transformations, as discussed in the previous section, are used to move objects between these coordinate systems. For example:

- **Model to World:** The model matrix transforms vertices from model space to world space.
- **World to View:** The view matrix transforms vertices from world space to view space.
- **View to Clip:** The projection matrix transforms vertices from view space to clip space.

Projections: From 3D to 2D

Projections are used to map the 3D scene onto a 2D screen or window. There are two main types of projections:

- **Perspective Projection:** Mimics how we see the world, with objects further away appearing smaller. This creates a sense of depth and realism.
- **Orthographic Projection:** Preserves parallel lines, making it useful for technical drawings and architectural visualizations.

Perspective Projection

In perspective projection, objects further from the camera appear smaller due to the converging lines of sight. The perspective projection matrix defines a viewing frustum, which is a truncated pyramid that determines the visible region of the scene. Objects outside this frustum are clipped.

Orthographic Projection

In orthographic projection, parallel lines remain parallel, and the size of objects does not change with distance. The orthographic projection matrix defines a viewing box, which is a rectangular region that determines the visible portion of the scene.

Projection Matrix in Shaders

The projection matrix is typically passed to the vertex shader as a uniform variable. The shader then multiplies this matrix with the vertex position to transform it to clip space.

Example: Defining a Perspective Projection Matrix

C++

```
glm::mat4 proj = glm::perspective(glm::radians(45.0f),
swapChainExtent.width                /                (float)
swapChainExtent.height, 0.1f, 10.0f);
```

This code uses the glm::perspective function to create a perspective projection matrix. The parameters define the field of view, aspect ratio, and near and far clipping planes.

Understanding the Viewport

The viewport defines the rectangular region of the screen where the final image is rendered. It maps the normalized coordinates of clip space to the pixel coordinates of the screen.

Depth in 3D Graphics

Depth information is crucial for correctly rendering 3D scenes. The depth buffer stores the distance of each pixel from the camera, allowing the graphics pipeline to determine which objects are in front of others and should be visible.

Coordinate Systems and Projections in Action

By understanding coordinate systems and projections, you gain a deeper understanding of how 3D scenes are transformed and rendered in Vulkan. This knowledge is essential for correctly positioning objects, setting up cameras, and achieving the desired visual effects in your applications.

Part II: Essential Vulkan Techniques

Chapter 5: Textures and Samplers

Image Objects and Memory Allocation

Textures breathe life into 3D graphics, adding detail, realism, and visual richness to your scenes. In Vulkan, textures are represented by image objects, which are versatile data structures that store image data in various formats and dimensions. Understanding how to create and manage these image objects, along with their underlying memory allocation, is essential for effectively utilizing textures in your Vulkan applications.

Image Objects: More Than Just Pictures

While we often associate images with visual representations like photographs or artwork, in Vulkan, image objects have a broader meaning. They can represent:

- **Color Textures:** Store color information that is mapped onto the surfaces of 3D models, adding detail and visual appeal.
- **Depth Textures:** Store depth information, used for depth testing and shadow mapping.
- **Stencil Textures:** Store stencil values, used for masking and special effects.

- **Render Targets:** Serve as the destination for rendering operations, allowing you to render to textures instead of directly to the screen.
- **General-Purpose Data:** Can be used to store arbitrary data that can be accessed and processed by shaders.

Creating Image Objects

Creating an image object involves specifying various parameters that define its characteristics:

- **Image Type:** 1D, 2D, or 3D, depending on the dimensionality of the image data.
- **Format:** The data format of the image, such as VK_FORMAT_R8G8B8A8_UNORM for an 8-bit-per-channel RGBA image.
- **Extent:** The width, height, and depth of the image.
- **Mip Levels:** The number of mipmap levels, which are pre-calculated, downsampled versions of the image used for efficient rendering at different distances.
- **Array Layers:** The number of layers in the image, used for texture arrays or cubemaps.
- **Usage:** How the image will be used, such as color attachment, depth attachment, or sampled image.

- **Tiling:** How the image data is laid out in memory, either linear or optimal for the GPU.

Memory Allocation for Images

Once you've defined the properties of your image object, you need to allocate memory for it. This involves:

1. **Determining Memory Requirements:** Use the vkGetImageMemoryRequirements function to determine the size and memory type requirements of the image.
2. **Finding a Suitable Memory Type:** Select a memory type that satisfies the requirements of the image, considering factors such as host visibility, device locality, and coherency.
3. **Allocating Memory:** Allocate a block of memory from the chosen memory type using the vkAllocateMemory function.
4. **Binding Memory:** Bind the allocated memory to the image object using the vkBindImageMemory function.

Layout Transitions

Image objects can exist in different layouts, which affect how the image data can be accessed and used. You need to perform layout transitions using pipeline barriers to ensure that the image is in the correct layout for the intended operation.

Code Example: Creating an Image Object and Allocating Memory

C++

```cpp
// Create image object

VkImageCreateInfo imageInfo{};

imageInfo.sType                              =
VK_STRUCTURE_TYPE_IMAGE_CREATE_INFO;

// ... other image parameters ...


VkImage image;

vkCreateImage(device, &imageInfo, nullptr, &image);


// Get memory requirements

VkMemoryRequirements memRequirements;

vkGetImageMemoryRequirements(device,        image,
&memRequirements);


// Allocate memory

VkMemoryAllocateInfo allocInfo{};
```

```
allocInfo.sType                                =
VK_STRUCTURE_TYPE_MEMORY_ALLOCATE_IN
FO;

allocInfo.allocationSize = memRequirements.size;

allocInfo.memoryTypeIndex                       =
findMemoryType(physicalDevice,
memRequirements.memoryTypeBits,
VK_MEMORY_PROPERTY_DEVICE_LOCAL_BIT);


VkDeviceMemory imageMemory;

vkAllocateMemory(device,       &allocInfo,      nullptr,
&imageMemory);


// Bind memory to image

vkBindImageMemory(device, image, imageMemory, 0);
```

This code snippet demonstrates the basic steps involved
in creating an image object and allocating memory for it.

Image Views

Image views provide a way to access specific portions or
aspects of an image object. They allow you to interpret

the image data in different ways, such as selecting a specific mip level, array layer, or format.

Populating Image Data

Once you've created an image object and allocated memory, you need to populate it with image data. This can be done through various methods, such as:

- **Staging Buffers:** Copy image data from a staging buffer in host-visible memory to the image in device-local memory.
- **Linear Tiling:** If the image is created with linear tiling, you can map the image memory to host memory and write the data directly.
- **Format Conversion:** Vulkan provides functions for converting between different image formats, allowing you to load images in various formats and convert them to the desired format.

By understanding the intricacies of image objects, memory allocation, and layout transitions, you can effectively utilize textures in your Vulkan applications, adding depth and visual richness to your 3D scenes.

Loading Image Data from Files

While procedurally generated textures or those created directly in memory have their uses, loading image data from files is essential for incorporating external assets into your Vulkan applications. This allows you to leverage the vast libraries of textures available in various formats, adding realism and detail to your virtual worlds.

Popular Image Formats

Several image formats are commonly used in game development and 3D graphics:

- **PNG (Portable Network Graphics):** A lossless format that supports transparency, making it suitable for UI elements, sprites, and textures with alpha channels.
- **JPEG (Joint Photographic Experts Group):** A lossy format that achieves high compression ratios, making it suitable for photographs and detailed textures where some loss of quality is acceptable.
- **TGA (Truevision TGA):** A versatile format that supports various color depths and compression options, often used for storing textures and image data in game development.
- **BMP (Bitmap):** A simple and widely supported format, often used for storing uncompressed image data.
- **DDS (DirectDraw Surface):** A format specifically designed for texture storage, supporting various compression techniques and mipmap generation.

Libraries for Image Loading

Several libraries simplify the process of loading image data from files:

- **stb_image:** A popular, header-only library that supports a wide range of image formats and provides a simple API for loading image data into memory.
- **FreeImage:** A powerful, open-source library that supports a vast number of image formats and provides advanced features like format conversion and image manipulation.
- **Vulkan Memory Allocator (VMA):** While primarily a memory allocation library, VMA also includes functions for loading image data from files and creating Vulkan image objects.

Steps for Loading Image Data

1. **Choose a Library:** Select an image loading library that suits your needs and integrate it into your project.
2. **Load Image Data:** Use the library's functions to load the image data from the file into a CPU-accessible buffer. This typically involves specifying the filename and retrieving the image's dimensions, format, and pixel data.

3. **Create a Staging Buffer:** Create a Vulkan buffer in host-visible memory and copy the loaded image data into this staging buffer.
4. **Create a Vulkan Image:** Create a Vulkan image object with the appropriate parameters based on the loaded image's dimensions and format.
5. **Transfer to Device Memory:** Use a transfer operation to copy the image data from the staging buffer to the Vulkan image in device-local memory. This ensures optimal access for the GPU.
6. **Generate Mipmaps (Optional):** If your image requires mipmaps, generate them either manually or using Vulkan's built-in mipmap generation capabilities.
7. **Create an Image View:** Create an image view to access the image data in your shaders.

Code Example: Loading an Image with stb_image

C++

```
// Load image data with stb_image

int texWidth, texHeight, texChannels;

stbi_uc* pixels = stbi_load("texture.jpg", &texWidth,
&texHeight, &texChannels, STBI_rgb_alpha);
```

```
// ... Create staging buffer and Vulkan image ...


// Copy image data to staging buffer

void* data;

vkMapMemory(device,      stagingBufferMemory,      0,
stagingBufferSize, 0, &data);

memcpy(data, pixels, imageSize);

vkUnmapMemory(device, stagingBufferMemory);


// ... Transfer data to Vulkan image ...


// Free image data loaded by stb_image

stbi_image_free(pixels);
```

This code snippet demonstrates how to load image data using stb_image and copy it to a Vulkan image.

Considerations

- **Image Format Conversion:** If the loaded image format doesn't match the desired format for your

Vulkan image, you might need to perform format conversion.

- **Gamma Correction:** Ensure that your image data is correctly gamma-corrected to avoid visual inconsistencies.
- **Texture Compression:** For larger textures, consider using texture compression formats like BC1, BC3, or ETC2 to reduce memory usage and improve performance.

By mastering the techniques for loading image data from files, you can seamlessly integrate external assets into your Vulkan applications, enriching your virtual worlds with diverse and detailed textures.

Samplers: Filtering and Addressing Modes

While image objects store the raw texture data, samplers define how this data is accessed and filtered when applied to 3D models. They act as intermediaries between the texture data and the shader, providing control over how texels (texture pixels) are sampled and interpolated.

Filtering: Smoothing the Way

Textures are often applied to surfaces that are viewed at varying distances and angles. When a texture is magnified or minified, filtering techniques are used to smooth out the appearance and avoid visual artifacts like pixelation or shimmering.

- **Magnification Filtering:** When a texture is magnified, meaning it appears larger on the screen than its original size, magnification filtering determines how texels are interpolated to fill the gaps between pixels. Common methods include:
  - **Nearest Neighbor:** Selects the texel closest to the sample point, resulting in a blocky appearance.
  - **Linear:** Interpolates between neighboring texels, producing a smoother result.
- **Minification Filtering:** When a texture is minified, meaning it appears smaller on the screen than its original size, minification filtering determines how multiple texels are combined to produce a single pixel value. Common methods include:
  - **Nearest Neighbor:** Selects the texel closest to the sample point, potentially causing aliasing artifacts.
  - **Linear:** Averages neighboring texels, reducing aliasing but potentially blurring the texture.
  - **Mipmapping:** Uses pre-calculated, downsampled versions of the texture (mipmaps) to select the most appropriate

level of detail for the current viewing distance, providing a good balance between performance and visual quality.

- ○ **Anisotropic Filtering:** A more advanced technique that samples texels along the direction of the surface, improving the appearance of textures on surfaces viewed at oblique angles.

Addressing Modes: Handling Texture Boundaries

Addressing modes define how texture coordinates outside the range of 0.0 to 1.0 are handled. They determine how the texture is sampled when the texture coordinates wrap around or extend beyond the edges of the texture image.

- **Repeat:** The texture repeats seamlessly in both the U (horizontal) and V (vertical) directions.
- **Mirrored Repeat:** The texture repeats in a mirrored fashion, creating a symmetrical pattern.
- **Clamp to Edge:** The texture coordinates are clamped to the edge of the texture image, extending the color of the edge pixels.
- **Clamp to Border:** The texture coordinates are clamped to a specified border color.

Creating Samplers

In Vulkan, you create sampler objects that encapsulate the desired filtering and addressing modes. These sampler objects are then used during rendering to sample textures.

Code Example: Creating a Sampler

```cpp
C++

VkSamplerCreateInfo samplerInfo{};

samplerInfo.sType                                    =
VK_STRUCTURE_TYPE_SAMPLER_CREATE_INF
O;

samplerInfo.magFilter = VK_FILTER_LINEAR;

samplerInfo.minFilter = VK_FILTER_LINEAR;

samplerInfo.addressModeU                             =
VK_SAMPLER_ADDRESS_MODE_REPEAT;

samplerInfo.addressModeV                             =
VK_SAMPLER_ADDRESS_MODE_REPEAT;

samplerInfo.addressModeW                             =
VK_SAMPLER_ADDRESS_MODE_REPEAT;

samplerInfo.anisotropyEnable = VK_TRUE;

samplerInfo.maxAnisotropy = 16;
```

```
samplerInfo.borderColor                          =
VK_BORDER_COLOR_INT_OPAQUE_BLACK;

samplerInfo.unnormalizedCoordinates = VK_FALSE;

// ... other sampler parameters ...


VkSampler sampler;

vkCreateSampler(device,      &samplerInfo,      nullptr,
&sampler);
```

This code snippet demonstrates how to create a sampler object with specific filtering and addressing modes.

Samplers in Shaders

Samplers are passed to shaders as uniform variables, allowing the shader to sample textures using the specified filtering and addressing modes.

Example: Sampling a Texture in a Shader

OpenGL Shading Language

```
#version 450
```

```
layout(binding = 1) uniform sampler2D texSampler;

void main() {

  vec4 color = texture(texSampler, texCoord);

  // ... use the sampled color ...

}
```

In this example, the texture function samples the texture using the provided sampler and texture coordinates.

Optimizing Texture Access

Choosing the right filtering and addressing modes can significantly impact the performance and visual quality of your textures. Consider the following factors:

- **Mipmapping:** Use mipmapping for textures that are viewed at varying distances to improve performance and reduce aliasing.
- **Anisotropic Filtering:** Enable anisotropic filtering for textures on surfaces viewed at oblique angles to improve their appearance.
- **Addressing Modes:** Choose addressing modes that suit the nature of your textures and the desired visual effect.

By understanding the role of samplers and their various parameters, you can fine-tune texture access in your Vulkan applications, achieving the desired balance between visual quality and performance.

Combining Textures: Multitexturing

Multitexturing is a powerful technique that allows you to combine multiple textures to create richer and more complex surface appearances. It opens up a world of possibilities for achieving realistic materials, intricate details, and stunning visual effects.

The Essence of Multitexturing

In its simplest form, multitexturing involves sampling multiple textures within a fragment shader and combining their color values to produce the final pixel color. This combination can be achieved through various blending operations, such as:

- **Linear Interpolation:** Blend textures based on a weighting factor, allowing for smooth transitions between different textures.
- **Multiplication:** Multiply the color values of the textures, useful for darkening or adding detail.
- **Addition:** Add the color values of the textures, useful for brightening or creating special effects.

- **Subtraction:** Subtract the color values of the textures, useful for creating masks or highlighting differences.

Applications of Multitexturing

Multitexturing has numerous applications in 3D graphics:

- **Detail Textures:** Combine a base texture with a detail texture to add fine details without increasing the resolution of the base texture.
- **Normal Mapping:** Use a normal map texture to perturb the surface normals, creating the illusion of surface detail without adding geometry.
- **Specular Mapping:** Use a specular map texture to control the shininess and reflectivity of different areas of a surface.
- **Ambient Occlusion:** Use an ambient occlusion map to simulate the self-shadowing that occurs in crevices and corners, adding depth and realism.
- **Light Mapping:** Use light maps to pre-calculate lighting information, reducing the need for real-time lighting calculations.

Texture Units and Samplers

To implement multitexturing in Vulkan, you utilize texture units and samplers.

- **Texture Units:** Logical units within the GPU that can be bound to different textures.
- **Samplers:** Define how the textures are sampled and filtered, as discussed in the previous section.

In your shader code, you access textures through their corresponding texture unit and sampler.

Code Example: Multitexturing in a Fragment Shader

OpenGL Shading Language

```
#version 450


layout(binding = 0) uniform sampler2D baseTexture;

layout(binding = 1) uniform sampler2D detailTexture;


void main() {

  vec4 baseColor = texture(baseTexture, texCoord);

  vec4 detailColor = texture(detailTexture, texCoord);


  vec4 finalColor = baseColor * detailColor; // Example:
Multiply textures
```

```
// ... other blending operations ...


fragColor = finalColor;

}
```

This code snippet demonstrates how to sample two textures in a fragment shader and combine their colors using multiplication.

Descriptor Sets and Bindings

To make multiple textures accessible to your shaders, you need to include them in your descriptor sets and define their bindings. This allows the shader to access the textures through their corresponding binding points.

Performance Considerations

While multitexturing offers great flexibility, it's important to be mindful of performance considerations:

- **Texture Unit Limits:** GPUs have a limited number of texture units, so avoid excessive texture sampling.

- **Memory Bandwidth:** Accessing multiple textures can increase memory bandwidth usage, potentially impacting performance.
- **Shader Complexity:** Complex blending operations in the shader can increase processing time.

Optimizations

- **Texture Atlases:** Combine multiple smaller textures into a single larger texture (atlas) to reduce texture unit usage and improve memory access patterns.
- **Texture Compression:** Use texture compression formats to reduce memory usage and improve performance.

By understanding the principles of multitexturing and utilizing Vulkan's texture units and samplers effectively, you can create stunningly detailed and realistic surfaces in your 3D scenes.

Chapter 6: Depth Testing and Stencil Operations

Depth Buffering: Solving Visibility Issues

When rendering a 3D scene, objects closer to the viewer should naturally occlude objects that are farther away. Without a mechanism to handle this, you might encounter situations where objects appear to be rendered in the wrong order, leading to visual artifacts and an incorrect perception of depth. This is where depth buffering comes to the rescue, providing an elegant solution to resolve visibility issues and ensure proper object occlusion.

The Depth Buffer: A Window into Distance

The depth buffer, also known as the z-buffer, is a special buffer that stores depth information for each pixel in the rendered image. This information represents the distance of that pixel from the viewer, typically measured in normalized device coordinates (NDC), where values range from 0.0 (near plane) to 1.0 (far plane).

How Depth Buffering Works

During the rendering process, the depth buffer is initialized with a default value, usually representing the maximum depth (1.0). As each fragment is processed, its depth value is compared to the corresponding value in the depth buffer.

- If the fragment's depth value is less than the value in the depth buffer (meaning it's closer to the viewer), the fragment's color is written to the color buffer, and its depth value is stored in the depth buffer, overwriting the previous value.
- If the fragment's depth value is greater than or equal to the value in the depth buffer (meaning it's farther away or at the same distance), the fragment is discarded, and the depth buffer remains unchanged.

This process ensures that only the closest fragments are visible, effectively resolving visibility conflicts and creating a correct perception of depth in the scene.

Enabling Depth Testing

In Vulkan, you enable depth testing by:

1. **Creating a Depth Image:** Create a Vulkan image object to serve as the depth buffer. This image should have the VK_IMAGE_USAGE_DEPTH_STENCIL_ATTACHMENT_BIT usage flag.
2. **Attaching the Depth Image to a Render Pass:** Include the depth image as a depth attachment in your render pass definition.

3. **Enabling Depth Testing in the Pipeline:** Enable depth testing and configure the depth comparison function (e.g., VK_COMPARE_OP_LESS or VK_COMPARE_OP_LESS_OR_EQUAL) in the pipeline's depth stencil state.

Depth Comparison Functions

Vulkan provides various depth comparison functions that determine how the fragment's depth is compared to the depth buffer value:

- VK_COMPARE_OP_NEVER: Never pass the depth test.
- VK_COMPARE_OP_LESS: Pass if the fragment's depth is less than the stored depth.
- VK_COMPARE_OP_EQUAL: Pass if the fragment's depth is equal to the stored depth.
- VK_COMPARE_OP_LESS_OR_EQUAL: Pass if the fragment's depth is less than or equal to the stored depth.
- VK_COMPARE_OP_GREATER: Pass if the fragment's depth is greater than the stored depth.
- VK_COMPARE_OP_NOT_EQUAL: Pass if the fragment's depth is not equal to the stored depth.
- VK_COMPARE_OP_GREATER_OR_EQUAL: Pass if the fragment's depth is greater than or equal to the stored depth.

- VK_COMPARE_OP_ALWAYS: Always pass the depth test.

Depth Write Mask

You can also control whether the depth buffer is updated using the depth write mask. This allows you to selectively write depth values, which can be useful for techniques like order-independent transparency.

Clearing the Depth Buffer

Before rendering a new frame, it's essential to clear the depth buffer to its default value. This ensures that the depth information from the previous frame doesn't interfere with the current frame's rendering.

Benefits of Depth Buffering

Depth buffering provides several benefits:

- **Correct Visibility:** Ensures that objects are rendered in the correct order, resolving occlusion issues.
- **Improved Realism:** Creates a more convincing sense of depth and spatial relationships in the scene.
- **Efficiency:** Avoids unnecessary rendering of occluded fragments, potentially improving performance.

By understanding the principles of depth buffering and how to configure it in Vulkan, you can create 3D scenes with accurate depth perception and proper object occlusion, enhancing the visual realism and immersion of your applications.

Depth Testing: Controlling Pixel Overdraw

While depth buffering provides a fundamental solution for visibility determination, depth testing offers finer control over how fragments are processed based on their depth values. This control allows you to optimize rendering performance by minimizing overdraw, which is the redundant rendering of pixels that are ultimately hidden by other objects.

The Depth Test

The depth test is a crucial step in the rendering pipeline that occurs after a fragment has been shaded but before it's written to the color buffer. During this test, the depth value of the incoming fragment is compared to the depth value already stored in the depth buffer at the corresponding pixel location. The outcome of this comparison, along with the depth comparison function and other settings, determines whether the fragment is discarded or allowed to proceed.

Depth Comparison Function

As mentioned earlier, Vulkan provides a variety of depth comparison functions, such as VK_COMPARE_OP_LESS, VK_COMPARE_OP_LESS_OR_EQUAL, VK_COMPARE_OP_GREATER, etc. These functions define the criteria for passing or failing the depth test. For example, VK_COMPARE_OP_LESS means that the fragment will only pass the test if its depth value is strictly less than the value in the depth buffer.

Depth Write Mask

The depth write mask allows you to control whether the depth buffer is updated during the depth test. By setting the depth write mask to VK_FALSE, you can prevent the fragment's depth value from being written to the depth buffer, even if it passes the depth test. This can be useful for techniques like order-independent transparency, where you want to blend transparent objects without affecting the depth buffer.

Early Depth Testing

Vulkan offers the capability to perform depth testing early in the pipeline, before fragment shading. This can significantly improve performance by avoiding unnecessary shading of fragments that would ultimately be discarded based on their depth. Early depth testing is particularly beneficial for scenes with high depth complexity, where many fragments are occluded.

Controlling Overdraw

Depth testing plays a vital role in controlling overdraw and optimizing rendering performance:

- **Choosing the Right Comparison Function:** Select a depth comparison function that suits your rendering needs. For most cases, VK_COMPARE_OP_LESS or VK_COMPARE_OP_LESS_OR_EQUAL is appropriate.
- **Early Depth Testing:** Enable early depth testing whenever possible to avoid shading occluded fragments.
- **Depth Write Mask:** Utilize the depth write mask to prevent unnecessary depth buffer updates, especially for transparent objects.
- **Z-Prepass:** For complex scenes, consider using a z-prepass rendering technique. This involves rendering the scene once with only depth information, followed by a second pass that performs full shading only for visible fragments.

Benefits of Controlling Overdraw

Minimizing overdraw offers several benefits:

- **Improved Performance:** Reduces the number of fragments that need to be shaded, freeing up GPU resources for other tasks.
- **Reduced Power Consumption:** Less fragment processing translates to lower power consumption, especially important for mobile and embedded devices.
- **Increased Frame Rates:** By optimizing rendering efficiency, you can achieve higher frame rates and smoother animation.

By understanding the nuances of depth testing and applying appropriate techniques to control overdraw, you can significantly enhance the performance of your Vulkan applications, especially in scenes with high depth complexity.

Stencil Buffering: Advanced Rendering Techniques

While depth buffering excels at resolving visibility based on distance, stencil buffering provides a versatile tool for achieving a wider range of effects by selectively controlling which fragments are rendered based on stencil values. This technique enables advanced rendering techniques that go beyond simple occlusion, opening up creative possibilities for visual effects and specialized rendering scenarios.

The Stencil Buffer: A Mask for Pixels

The stencil buffer is another special buffer, similar to the depth buffer, that stores an integer stencil value for each pixel in the rendered image. This value can be used as a mask to determine whether a fragment should be rendered or discarded.

Stencil Operations

Vulkan provides a rich set of stencil operations that allow you to manipulate stencil values during the rendering process. These operations include:

- **Keep:** Keep the current stencil value.
- **Zero:** Set the stencil value to zero.
- **Replace:** Replace the stencil value with a reference value.
- **Increment and Clamp:** Increment the stencil value, clamping it to a maximum value.
- **Decrement and Clamp:** Decrement the stencil value, clamping it to a minimum value.
- **Invert:** Invert the bits of the stencil value.
- **Increment and Wrap:** Increment the stencil value, wrapping around to zero if it exceeds the maximum value.
- **Decrement and Wrap:** Decrement the stencil value, wrapping around to the maximum value if it falls below zero.

Stencil Test

The stencil test compares the stencil value of the incoming fragment with a reference value using a comparison function. The outcome of this test, along with the stencil operations, determines how the stencil buffer is updated and whether the fragment is rendered.

Stencil Comparison Functions

Vulkan offers the same set of comparison functions for the stencil test as for the depth test, including VK_COMPARE_OP_NEVER, VK_COMPARE_OP_LESS, VK_COMPARE_OP_EQUAL, etc. These functions define the criteria for passing or failing the stencil test.

Two-Sided Stencil Operations

Vulkan allows you to specify different stencil operations for front-facing and back-facing polygons. This enables techniques like rendering outlines or highlighting specific edges of objects.

Applications of Stencil Buffering

Stencil buffering enables a variety of advanced rendering techniques:

- **Planar Reflections:** Create reflections by rendering the scene to a stencil buffer, then using the stencil values to mask out areas where the reflection should appear.
- **Shadow Volumes:** Generate shadows by extruding geometry from objects towards the light source and using stencil operations to determine shadowed areas.
- **Outlines:** Render outlines around objects by drawing the objects twice, once with a slightly larger scale and different stencil operations to highlight the edges.
- **Decals:** Apply decals to surfaces by rendering the decal geometry with stencil operations that restrict rendering to the desired area.
- **Post-Processing Effects:** Use stencil values to selectively apply post-processing effects to specific regions of the screen.

Code Example: Basic Stencil Operations

```cpp
C++

// ... Create depth/stencil image and attach to render pass
...




// Configure stencil operations in pipeline depth stencil
state
```

```
VkPipelineDepthStencilStateCreateInfo depthStencil{};

depthStencil.sType                        =
VK_STRUCTURE_TYPE_PIPELINE_DEPTH_STEN
CIL_STATE_CREATE_INFO;

depthStencil.depthTestEnable = VK_TRUE;

depthStencil.depthWriteEnable = VK_TRUE;

depthStencil.depthCompareOp               =
VK_COMPARE_OP_LESS;

depthStencil.stencilTestEnable = VK_TRUE;

depthStencil.front.compareOp              =
VK_COMPARE_OP_ALWAYS;

depthStencil.front.failOp = VK_STENCIL_OP_KEEP;

depthStencil.front.passOp                 =
VK_STENCIL_OP_REPLACE;

// ... other stencil operations ...
```

This code snippet demonstrates how to configure basic stencil operations in the pipeline's depth stencil state.

Combining Depth and Stencil

Depth and stencil buffering can be used together to achieve even more complex effects. For example, you can use depth testing to determine visibility and stencil operations to selectively modify or discard fragments based on specific criteria.

By mastering the techniques of stencil buffering, you can unlock a new level of creative control over your rendering process, achieving sophisticated visual effects and specialized rendering scenarios that go beyond the capabilities of depth buffering alone.

Early Depth Testing for Performance Optimization

As you've seen, depth testing is essential for determining fragment visibility. However, the traditional placement of the depth test in the rendering pipeline can lead to wasted processing. Early depth testing offers a performance optimization technique by moving the depth test earlier in the pipeline, potentially saving valuable GPU resources.

Traditional Depth Testing

In the traditional rendering pipeline, depth testing occurs after fragment shading. This means that even fragments that will ultimately be discarded due to depth occlusion still undergo the computationally expensive fragment shading process. This can be inefficient, especially in scenes with high depth complexity where many fragments are occluded.

Early Depth Testing

Early depth testing, as the name suggests, performs the depth test before fragment shading. This allows the pipeline to discard occluded fragments early on, avoiding the cost of shading them. Only fragments that pass the depth test proceed to the fragment shader, saving valuable GPU cycles.

Enabling Early Depth Testing in Vulkan

To enable early depth testing in Vulkan, you need to set the depthTestEnable and depthWriteEnable members of the VkPipelineDepthStencilStateCreateInfo structure to VK_TRUE and specify the desired depth comparison function. Additionally, you need to set the earlyFragmentTests member of the VkSubpassDependency structure to VK_TRUE when defining the subpass dependencies in your render pass.

Benefits of Early Depth Testing

- **Reduced Fragment Shading:** Avoids shading fragments that would be discarded due to depth occlusion, saving GPU resources.

- **Improved Performance:** Can lead to significant performance gains, especially in scenes with high depth complexity or expensive fragment shaders.
- **Lower Power Consumption:** Less fragment processing translates to lower power consumption.

When to Use Early Depth Testing

Early depth testing is generally beneficial in most scenarios, especially when:

- Your scene has high depth complexity, with many objects occluding each other.
- Your fragment shaders are computationally expensive.
- You are targeting performance-constrained devices, such as mobile or embedded systems.

Caveats

While early depth testing offers performance advantages, there are a few caveats to consider:

- **Order Dependency:** Early depth testing can affect the rendering order of fragments, potentially leading to issues with techniques that rely on specific fragment ordering, such as order-independent transparency.

- **Shader Side Effects:** If your fragment shader has side effects, such as writing to image buffers or atomic counters, these effects might not be executed for fragments discarded by early depth testing.

Balancing Performance and Correctness

When utilizing early depth testing, it's crucial to balance performance optimization with the correctness of your rendering. Carefully consider the potential impact on fragment ordering and shader side effects, and adjust your rendering techniques accordingly if necessary.

By understanding the benefits and caveats of early depth testing, you can make informed decisions about when and how to utilize this optimization technique in your Vulkan applications, maximizing rendering efficiency without compromising visual fidelity.

Chapter 7: Rendering with Multiple Objects

Descriptor Sets and Layouts

As your Vulkan applications grow in complexity, you'll inevitably need to render scenes with multiple objects, each potentially having unique textures, materials, and transformation parameters. Managing these diverse resources and efficiently supplying them to your shaders can become a challenge. This is where descriptor sets and layouts come into play, offering a powerful mechanism for organizing and binding shader resources.

Descriptor Sets: Bundling Resources

Descriptor sets act as containers for the various resources that your shaders need to access. These resources can include:

- **Uniform Buffers:** Hold constant data that remains the same for multiple vertices or fragments, such as transformation matrices, lighting parameters, or material properties.
- **Sampled Images:** Represent textures that are sampled by the shader to provide color, normal, or other surface information.
- **Samplers:** Define how the sampled images are filtered and accessed.

- **Storage Buffers:** Provide read-write access to buffers from your shaders, enabling dynamic data exchange between the CPU and GPU.
- **Storage Images:** Allow shaders to read and write to image data, enabling techniques like compute shaders and image processing.

By grouping related resources into descriptor sets, you create logical bundles that can be easily bound to your shaders, streamlining resource management and improving rendering efficiency.

Descriptor Set Layouts: Defining the Blueprint

Before you can create descriptor sets, you need to define their layout. A descriptor set layout acts as a blueprint that specifies:

- **Number of Bindings:** The number of resources that the descriptor set will hold.
- **Binding Types:** The type of each resource, such as uniform buffer, sampled image, or sampler.
- **Shader Stages:** Which shader stages will access each resource (vertex, fragment, or compute).

The descriptor set layout ensures that your shaders and descriptor sets are compatible, providing a clear definition of the resources that will be available to the shader.

Creating Descriptor Sets and Layouts

To create a descriptor set layout, you use the vkCreateDescriptorSetLayout function, providing a VkDescriptorSetLayoutCreateInfo structure that specifies the layout bindings.

Once you have a descriptor set layout, you can create descriptor sets from a descriptor pool using the vkAllocateDescriptorSets function. The descriptor pool acts as a memory allocator for descriptor sets, allowing you to efficiently manage their allocation and deallocation.

Updating Descriptor Sets

After creating descriptor sets, you need to populate them with the actual resources (buffers, images, samplers) that your shaders will use. This is done using the vkUpdateDescriptorSets function, which allows you to write descriptor information to the descriptor sets.

Binding Descriptor Sets

Finally, to make the resources available to your shaders, you bind the descriptor sets to the graphics pipeline using the vkCmdBindDescriptorSets function. This associates the descriptor sets with the current pipeline, allowing the shaders to access the resources through their defined binding points.

Code Example: Creating and Using Descriptor Sets

C++

```cpp
// Define descriptor set layout binding

VkDescriptorSetLayoutBinding uboLayoutBinding{};

uboLayoutBinding.binding = 0;

uboLayoutBinding.descriptorType                =
VK_DESCRIPTOR_TYPE_UNIFORM_BUFFER;

uboLayoutBinding.descriptorCount = 1;

uboLayoutBinding.stageFlags                     =
VK_SHADER_STAGE_VERTEX_BIT;


// Create descriptor set layout

VkDescriptorSetLayoutCreateInfo layoutInfo{};

layoutInfo.sType                                =
VK_STRUCTURE_TYPE_DESCRIPTOR_SET_LAYO
UT_CREATE_INFO;

layoutInfo.bindingCount = 1;

layoutInfo.pBindings = &uboLayoutBinding;
```

```
VkDescriptorSetLayout descriptorSetLayout;

vkCreateDescriptorSetLayout(device,      &layoutInfo,
nullptr, &descriptorSetLayout);


// ... Create descriptor pool and allocate descriptor set ...


// Update descriptor set with uniform buffer handle

// ... (refer to previous example) ...


// Bind descriptor set

vkCmdBindDescriptorSets(commandBuffer,
VK_PIPELINE_BIND_POINT_GRAPHICS,
pipelineLayout, 0, 1, &descriptorSet, 0, nullptr);
```

This code snippet illustrates how to create a descriptor set layout, allocate a descriptor set, update it with a uniform buffer handle, and bind it to the graphics pipeline.

Benefits of Descriptor Sets and Layouts

Descriptor sets and layouts offer several benefits:

- **Organization:** Provide a structured way to manage shader resources, improving code clarity and maintainability.
- **Efficiency:** Reduce resource binding overhead by grouping related resources into sets.
- **Flexibility:** Allow for dynamic updates of resources between draw calls, enabling efficient rendering of scenes with varying materials and parameters.

By understanding the concepts of descriptor sets and layouts, you can effectively manage shader resources in your Vulkan applications, enabling you to render complex scenes with multiple objects and diverse materials.

Push Constants: Efficient Per-Object Data

While uniform buffers excel at handling constant data shared by multiple objects, push constants provide an even more efficient way to supply small amounts of per-object data to your shaders. They offer a streamlined mechanism for updating shader parameters without the overhead of managing descriptor sets and bindings.

What are Push Constants?

Push constants are small data packets that are "pushed" directly to the shader stages during command buffer recording. This data is stored in a dedicated memory region accessible to the shader, bypassing the need for descriptor sets and allowing for immediate updates without the latency of memory transfers.

Benefits of Push Constants

- **Efficiency:** Push constants are extremely efficient for updating small amounts of shader data, as they avoid the overhead of descriptor set management and memory transfers.
- **Simplicity:** Using push constants simplifies your code by eliminating the need for descriptor set layouts, allocations, and updates.
- **Flexibility:** Push constants can be updated frequently and dynamically, making them ideal for per-object parameters that change often.

Limitations of Push Constants

- **Size Limits:** The amount of data you can pass as push constants is limited by the hardware. Vulkan specifies a minimum size of 128 bytes, but the actual limit may vary depending on the device.
- **Scope:** Push constants are limited to a single shader stage or a consecutive range of shader stages. You cannot share push constants between unrelated shader stages.

Using Push Constants

To use push constants, you need to:

1. **Define Push Constant Ranges:** During pipeline layout creation, specify the push constant ranges for each shader stage. This defines the size and offset of the push constant data within the dedicated memory region.
2. **Push Constant Data:** Use the vkCmdPushConstants function to push the data to the shader stages during command buffer recording.
3. **Access in Shaders:** In your shader code, declare a push_constant block to access the pushed data.

Code Example: Using Push Constants

C++

```
// Define push constant range

VkPushConstantRange pushConstantRange{};

pushConstantRange.stageFlags                    =
VK_SHADER_STAGE_VERTEX_BIT;

pushConstantRange.offset = 0;

pushConstantRange.size = sizeof(PushConstantData);


// Create pipeline layout with push constant range
```

```cpp
VkPipelineLayoutCreateInfo pipelineLayoutInfo{};

// ... other pipeline layout parameters ...

pipelineLayoutInfo.pushConstantRangeCount = 1;

pipelineLayoutInfo.pPushConstantRanges      =
&pushConstantRange;


VkPipelineLayout pipelineLayout;

vkCreatePipelineLayout(device,    &pipelineLayoutInfo,
nullptr, &pipelineLayout);


// ... In command buffer recording ...


// Push constant data

PushConstantData pushData{};

// ... populate pushData ...

vkCmdPushConstants(commandBuffer,  pipelineLayout,
VK_SHADER_STAGE_VERTEX_BIT,                    0,
sizeof(PushConstantData), &pushData);


// ... In vertex shader ...
```

```
layout(push_constant) uniform PushConstantBlock {

  // ... push constant members ...

} pushConstants;


// Access push constant data

vec3 color = pushConstants.color;
```

This code snippet demonstrates how to define a push constant range, push data to the vertex shader, and access it within the shader code.

Use Cases for Push Constants

Push constants are well-suited for various scenarios:

- **Per-Object Transformations:** Pass individual model matrices for each object.
- **Material Parameters:** Supply per-object material properties like color or reflectivity.
- **Instance Data:** Provide unique data for each instance in instanced rendering.
- **Shader Toggles:** Pass flags or parameters to enable or disable specific shader features.

Choosing Between Uniform Buffers and Push Constants

When deciding between uniform buffers and push constants, consider the following:

- **Data Size:** For small amounts of data (within the push constant size limit), push constants are generally more efficient.
- **Frequency of Updates:** If the data changes frequently, push constants offer a more streamlined approach.
- **Sharing Between Shader Stages:** If the data needs to be shared between unrelated shader stages, uniform buffers are necessary.

By understanding the strengths and limitations of push constants, you can effectively utilize them to optimize data transfer to your shaders, improving the performance and efficiency of your Vulkan applications.

Instancing: Drawing Many Objects Efficiently

In many 3D applications, you often need to render a large number of similar objects, such as trees in a forest, grass blades in a field, or particles in an explosion. Drawing each of these objects individually can lead to significant performance overhead due to the repeated draw calls and state changes. Instancing offers a powerful optimization technique to address this challenge, allowing you to render multiple instances of the same object with a single draw call, dramatically improving rendering efficiency.

The Concept of Instancing

Instancing leverages the fact that many objects in a scene share the same underlying geometry but may have different transformations, materials, or other attributes. Instead of issuing separate draw calls for each instance, you provide the GPU with an array of per-instance data, and the vertex shader uses this data to transform and render each instance individually.

Benefits of Instancing

- **Reduced Draw Calls:** Significantly reduces the number of draw calls, minimizing CPU overhead and improving rendering performance.
- **Efficient Data Transfer:** Transfers per-instance data to the GPU efficiently, avoiding redundant transfers of the same geometry data.
- **Flexibility:** Allows for variations in transformations, materials, or other attributes for each instance, enabling diverse and dynamic scenes.

Implementing Instancing in Vulkan

To implement instancing in Vulkan, you need to:

1. **Provide Per-Instance Data:** Create a buffer to store per-instance data, such as transformation matrices, colors, or other attributes. This buffer can be a vertex buffer or a storage buffer, depending on how you access the data in your shader.

2. **Enable Instancing in the Pipeline:** During pipeline creation, enable instancing by setting the VkPipelineVertexInputStateCreateInfo structure's instance member to a value greater than zero. This specifies the number of instances to draw with each draw call.

3. **Access Instance Data in the Shader:** In your vertex shader, access the per-instance data using the built-in gl_InstanceIndex variable. This variable provides the index of the current instance being processed.

Code Example: Instanced Rendering

```cpp
C++

// ... Create buffer for per-instance data ...


// Enable instancing in pipeline creation
```

```
VkPipelineVertexInputStateCreateInfo
vertexInputInfo{};

// ... other vertex input state parameters ...

vertexInputInfo.instance = 1; // Enable instancing


// ... In vertex shader ...


layout(location = 2) in mat4 instanceMatrix; //
Per-instance matrix


void main() {

  mat4 modelMatrix = instanceMatrix[gl_InstanceIndex];

  // ... use modelMatrix to transform the vertex ...

}
```

This code snippet demonstrates how to enable instancing in the pipeline and access per-instance matrices in the vertex shader.

Instancing with Different Attributes

You can extend instancing to handle variations in other attributes, such as color or texture coordinates. Simply add the necessary attributes to your per-instance data buffer and access them in the shader using gl_InstanceIndex.

Optimizations

- **Instanced Arrays:** For large numbers of instances, consider using instanced arrays, which allow you to draw multiple instances with a single draw call and a single set of per-instance data.
- **Multi-Draw Indirect:** If you have multiple sets of instanced data, use multi-draw indirect rendering to draw them all with a single dispatch call, further reducing CPU overhead.

Use Cases for Instancing

Instancing is particularly beneficial for rendering:

- **Large Crowds:** Render hundreds or thousands of characters with unique animations and appearances.
- **Vegetation:** Create realistic forests, grasslands, or other natural environments with numerous instances of trees, plants, and foliage.

- **Particle Systems:** Render particle effects like explosions, smoke, or fire with thousands of individual particles.
- **Repeating Patterns:** Efficiently render repeating patterns like tiles, bricks, or fences.

By mastering the technique of instancing, you can significantly enhance the performance of your Vulkan applications when rendering scenes with large numbers of similar objects. This optimization allows you to create rich and dynamic environments without sacrificing frame rates or visual fidelity.

Scene Hierarchies and Transformations

As your 3D scenes become more elaborate, managing individual objects and their transformations can become cumbersome. Scene hierarchies provide a powerful organizational structure for arranging objects in a parent-child relationship, enabling efficient and intuitive manipulation of complex scenes.

The Essence of Scene Hierarchies

A scene hierarchy, also known as a scene graph, represents a scene as a tree-like structure where objects are organized in a parent-child relationship. Each object in the hierarchy is called a node, and each node can have one parent and multiple children.

This hierarchical structure allows you to group related objects, such as the parts of a car or the limbs of a character, under a common parent. Transformations applied to a parent node are automatically inherited by its children, enabling coordinated movement and animation.

Benefits of Scene Hierarchies

- **Organization:** Provides a clear and structured way to organize complex scenes, making them easier to manage and understand.
- **Efficiency:** Enables efficient transformation of groups of objects by applying transformations to parent nodes.
- **Modularity:** Promotes modularity by allowing you to create reusable components or sub-hierarchies.
- **Animation:** Facilitates animation by manipulating transformations of parent nodes to create coordinated movements.

Transformations in Hierarchies

Each node in a scene hierarchy has its own local transformation, which defines its position, orientation, and scale relative to its parent. When rendering an object, its final transformation is calculated by concatenating the transformations of all its ancestors in the hierarchy.

For example, consider a car model with a wheel as a child node. Rotating the car node will also rotate the wheel, as the wheel inherits the car's transformation. Additionally, rotating the wheel node will rotate the wheel around its own local axis, relative to the car's orientation.

Implementing Scene Hierarchies

You can implement scene hierarchies in your Vulkan applications by:

1. **Representing Nodes:** Create a data structure to represent nodes in the hierarchy, storing their local transformations and pointers to their parent and children.
2. **Traversing the Hierarchy:** Implement a function to traverse the hierarchy, calculating the final transformation matrix for each object by concatenating the transformations of its ancestors.
3. **Passing Transformations to Shaders:** Pass the calculated transformation matrices to your shaders as uniform variables.

Code Example: Scene Hierarchy Traversal

C++

```cpp
glm::mat4 getNodeTransform(Node* node) {
  glm::mat4 transform = node->localTransform;
  Node* parent = node->parent;
  while (parent != nullptr) {
    transform = parent->localTransform * transform;
    parent = parent->parent;
  }
  return transform;
}
```

This code snippet demonstrates a simple function to calculate the final transformation matrix for a given node by traversing its ancestors in the hierarchy.

Scene Hierarchies in Action

Scene hierarchies are widely used in various 3D applications:

- **Character Animation:** Represent characters with a hierarchy of bones and joints, enabling realistic skeletal animation.
- **Mechanical Systems:** Model complex mechanical systems with interconnected parts, such as robots or vehicles.
- **Level Design:** Organize game levels with hierarchical structures, grouping related objects and simplifying level management.
- **Procedural Generation:** Generate complex scenes procedurally by creating hierarchical structures of objects.

By utilizing scene hierarchies and their inherent transformation capabilities, you can effectively manage and manipulate complex 3D scenes in your Vulkan applications, enabling efficient rendering, intuitive animation, and organized scene structure.

Chapter 8: Lighting and Shading

Basic Lighting Models: Ambient, Diffuse, and Specular

Lighting plays a crucial role in breathing life into 3D scenes, transforming them from flat and lifeless collections of polygons into vibrant and believable worlds.[1] By simulating the interaction of light with surfaces, we can achieve a sense of depth, realism, and visual appeal.[2] This section explores the fundamental lighting models – ambient, diffuse, and specular – that form the foundation of lighting calculations in computer graphics.[3]

Ambient Lighting: A Gentle Glow

Ambient lighting represents the overall background illumination present in a scene, regardless of the direction or position of light sources.[4] It simulates the indirect scattering of light that bounces off various surfaces, creating a soft and omnipresent glow.[5]

In its simplest form, ambient lighting is calculated as:

Ambient Color = Object Color * Ambient Light Intensity

This calculation multiplies the object's base color by the intensity of the ambient light, resulting in a subtle illumination that affects all surfaces equally.

Diffuse Lighting: Simulating Surface Scattering

Diffuse lighting simulates the scattering of light that occurs when light rays hit a matte surface. This type of lighting depends on the angle between the surface normal and the direction of the light source.[6]

The intensity of diffuse lighting is calculated using Lambert's cosine law:[7]

Diffuse Color = Object Color * Light Color * max(0, dot(Normal, Light Direction))

This calculation takes into account the object's color, the light's color, and the dot product between the surface normal and the light direction. The max(0, ...) function ensures that surfaces facing away from the light receive no diffuse illumination.

Specular Lighting: Highlights and Shine

Specular lighting simulates the highlights that appear on shiny surfaces when light reflects directly towards the viewer.[8] This type of lighting depends on the angle between the reflected light vector and the view direction.

The intensity of specular lighting is often calculated using the Phong reflection model:

Specular Color = Light Color * Specular Color * pow(max(0, dot(Reflected Light, View Direction)), Shininess)

This calculation considers the light's color, the object's specular color, and the dot product between the reflected light vector and the view direction. The pow(...) function raises this dot product to a power determined by the shininess exponent, controlling the size and intensity of the specular highlight.

Combining Lighting Components

To achieve a more realistic lighting effect, you typically combine the ambient, diffuse, and specular components:

Final Color = Ambient Color + Diffuse Color + Specular Color

This combination creates a layered lighting effect that captures the subtle nuances of light interaction with surfaces.

Implementing Lighting in Shaders

Lighting calculations are typically performed in the fragment shader. You pass the necessary parameters, such as light positions, colors, and intensities, as uniform variables to the shader.[9] The shader then calculates the lighting contributions for each fragment based on the surface normal, view direction, and light direction.

Beyond Basic Lighting

While the ambient, diffuse, and specular models provide a solid foundation, more advanced lighting techniques exist:

- **Attenuation:** Simulates the decrease in light intensity with distance.
- **Multiple Lights:** Calculates the contributions of multiple light sources.
- **Shadows:** Incorporates shadows to enhance realism and depth perception.[10]
- **Normal Mapping:** Uses normal maps to simulate surface detail and enhance lighting effects.[11]

- **Physically Based Rendering (PBR):** Employs more physically accurate lighting models for realistic material representation.[12]

By understanding the basic lighting models and how to implement them in your Vulkan shaders, you can create compelling 3D scenes with realistic lighting and shading, enhancing the visual appeal and immersion of your applications.

Implementing Lighting in Shaders

As a tech expert and author, you understand that lighting calculations are typically handled within shaders, specifically the fragment shader. This allows for precise control over the lighting at each pixel, enabling a wide range of effects and styles. Let's explore how to implement lighting calculations in your Vulkan shaders.

Passing Lighting Data to Shaders

Before you can perform lighting calculations, you need to provide the necessary data to your shaders. This data is typically passed as uniform variables and can include:

- **Light properties:**
    - Position (for directional, point, and spotlights)
    - Direction (for directional lights)
    - Color

- ○ Intensity
- ○ Attenuation factors (for point and spotlights)
- ○ Cone angles (for spotlights)
- **Material properties:**
  - ○ Ambient color
  - ○ Diffuse color
  - ○ Specular color
  - ○ Shininess exponent

You can organize this data into structs in your C++ code and then pass them to the shader as uniform buffer objects.

Calculating Lighting in the Fragment Shader

Within your fragment shader, you'll receive the interpolated vertex attributes, such as position, normal, and texture coordinates. You'll also have access to the lighting and material data passed as uniforms. Using this information, you can implement the lighting equations discussed in the previous section.

Example Fragment Shader with Lighting

OpenGL Shading Language

#version 450

```glsl
layout(location = 0) in vec3 fragColor;

layout(location = 1) in vec3 fragNormal;

layout(location = 2) in vec3 fragPos;


layout(binding = 0) uniform UniformBufferObject {
    mat4 view;
    mat4 proj;
    vec3 viewPos; // Camera position
    Light light;  // Light properties
} ubo;


layout(location = 0) out vec4 outColor;


void main() {
    // Ambient
    vec3 ambient = light.ambient * fragColor;


    // Diffuse
```

```glsl
vec3 lightDir = normalize(light.position - fragPos);
float diff = max(dot(fragNormal, lightDir), 0.0);
vec3 diffuse = light.diffuse * diff * fragColor;


// Specular
vec3 viewDir = normalize(ubo.viewPos - fragPos);
vec3 reflectDir = reflect(-lightDir, fragNormal);
float spec = pow(max(dot(viewDir, reflectDir), 0.0), 32);
vec3 specular = light.specular * spec * fragColor;


vec3 result = ambient + diffuse + specular;
outColor = vec4(result, 1.0);
}
```

This fragment shader example demonstrates how to calculate ambient, diffuse, and specular lighting contributions and combine them to produce the final fragment color.

Optimizations

- **Pre-calculate values:** If certain lighting parameters remain constant, pre-calculate them on the CPU and pass them as uniforms to avoid redundant calculations in the shader.
- **Normalize vectors:** Normalize vectors only once if they are used multiple times in the calculations.
- **Branching:** Minimize branching in shaders as it can hinder performance.

Advanced Lighting Techniques

You can extend this basic lighting implementation with more advanced techniques:

- **Attenuation:** Apply attenuation factors to simulate the decrease in light intensity with distance.
- **Multiple Lights:** Loop through multiple light sources and accumulate their contributions.
- **Shadows:** Implement shadow mapping or other shadowing techniques to enhance realism.
- **Normal Mapping:** Use normal maps to perturb the surface normals and create the illusion of finer details.

By implementing lighting calculations in your Vulkan shaders and exploring advanced techniques, you can create visually stunning and immersive 3D scenes with realistic lighting and shading.

Normal Mapping: Adding Surface Detail

Normal mapping is a powerful technique that enhances the visual detail of your 3D models without increasing their geometric complexity. It allows you to simulate intricate surface features like bumps, grooves, and wrinkles by modifying the surface normals used in lighting calculations. This creates the illusion of depth and texture, making your models appear more realistic and engaging.

The Role of Normals in Lighting

Surface normals play a crucial role in determining how light interacts with a surface. They define the orientation of the surface at each point, influencing the calculation of diffuse and specular lighting. By modifying the normals, you can alter the way light reflects off the surface, creating the appearance of bumps and depressions.

Normal Maps: Encoded Normal Information

A normal map is a special texture that stores normal vectors in its RGB channels. Each pixel in the normal map, called a texel, represents a normal vector that deviates from the original surface normal of the 3D model. These deviations create the illusion of surface detail when used in lighting calculations.

Creating Normal Maps

Normal maps are typically generated from high-resolution 3D models or sculpted surfaces. The normal vectors from the high-resolution model are baked into a texture, which can then be applied to a lower-resolution model to add detail.

Tangent Space

Normal maps are often stored in tangent space, which is a coordinate system that is aligned with the surface of the 3D model. This makes it easier to apply the normal map to different parts of the model without distortions.

Implementing Normal Mapping in Shaders

To implement normal mapping in your Vulkan shaders, you need to:

1. **Load the Normal Map:** Load the normal map texture into your application.
2. **Calculate the TBN Matrix:** In the vertex shader, calculate the tangent, bitangent, and normal vectors for each vertex and construct a TBN

matrix that transforms vectors from tangent space to world space.

3. **Sample the Normal Map:** In the fragment shader, sample the normal map using the interpolated texture coordinates.

4. **Transform the Normal:** Transform the sampled normal vector from tangent space to world space using the TBN matrix.

5. **Use the Normal in Lighting Calculations:** Use the transformed normal vector in your lighting calculations to determine the diffuse and specular contributions.

Code Example: Normal Mapping in a Fragment Shader

OpenGL Shading Language

```
#version 450


// ... input variables and uniforms ...


void main() {

  // ... sample normal map ...
```

```
// Transform normal from tangent space to world space

    vec3 normal = normalize(texture(normalMap,
texCoord).rgb * 2.0 - 1.0);

 normal = normalize(tbn * normal);


// ... use normal in lighting calculations ...

}
```

Benefits of Normal Mapping

- **Enhanced Visual Detail:** Adds intricate surface details without increasing geometric complexity.
- **Improved Performance:** Less geometry to process leads to improved rendering performance.
- **Reduced Memory Usage:** Normal maps typically require less memory than storing high-resolution geometry.

Applications of Normal Mapping

Normal mapping is widely used in various 3D applications:

- **Game Development:** Adds detail to characters, environments, and objects.
- **Film and Animation:** Creates realistic surfaces and textures for characters and props.
- **Visualization:** Enhances the visual appeal of scientific and medical visualizations.

By understanding and implementing normal mapping in your Vulkan applications, you can significantly enhance the visual fidelity of your 3D models without sacrificing performance. This technique adds a level of realism and detail that brings your scenes to life.

Advanced Shading Techniques

As a seasoned tech expert, you know that basic lighting models provide a solid foundation, but to truly capture the nuances of light and material interaction, advanced shading techniques are essential. Let's explore some of these techniques that can elevate the realism and visual appeal of your Vulkan applications.

1. Physically Based Rendering (PBR)

PBR aims to model the interaction of light with surfaces in a physically accurate manner, resulting in more realistic and believable materials. Key concepts in PBR include:

- **Microfacet Theory:** Models surfaces as a collection of tiny microfacets, each with its own orientation and reflective properties.
- **Energy Conservation:** Ensures that the total amount of reflected light never exceeds the incoming light energy.
- **Metallic and Roughness:** Uses metallic and roughness parameters to control the material's reflective properties.
- **BRDF (Bidirectional Reflectance Distribution Function):** Describes how light is reflected from a surface based on its incoming and outgoing directions.

PBR shaders often utilize complex BRDF functions, such as the Cook-Torrance BRDF, to accurately calculate light reflection.

2. Image-Based Lighting (IBL)

IBL uses environment maps to capture the surrounding lighting conditions and reflections, creating more realistic and immersive environments. Key components of IBL include:

- **Environment Maps:** Cubemaps or spherical maps that capture the surrounding environment.

- **Irradiance Maps:** Pre-computed maps that store the diffuse lighting information from the environment.
- **Reflection Probes:** Capture reflections of the environment from specific points in the scene.

IBL shaders use these maps to approximate the global illumination and reflections, adding a sense of depth and realism to the scene.

3. Subsurface Scattering

Subsurface scattering simulates the way light penetrates translucent materials and scatters beneath the surface before exiting. This effect is crucial for rendering materials like skin, wax, or jade.

Subsurface scattering shaders approximate this effect by sampling the material at multiple points beneath the surface and accumulating the scattered light contributions.

4. Ambient Occlusion

Ambient occlusion (AO) simulates the self-shadowing that occurs in crevices and corners of objects, adding depth and realism to the scene.

AO shaders approximate this effect by calculating the amount of ambient light that reaches each point on the surface, taking into account the surrounding geometry. Techniques like screen-space ambient occlusion (SSAO) offer efficient ways to calculate AO in real-time.

5. Parallax Mapping

Parallax mapping enhances the illusion of depth in textures by displacing the texture coordinates based on the view direction. This creates the impression that surface details are actually raised or recessed.

Parallax mapping shaders use a height map to determine the displacement of the texture coordinates, creating a more convincing sense of depth and parallax.

6. Tessellation

Tessellation allows you to dynamically subdivide polygons into smaller triangles, increasing the geometric detail of your models. This can be used to create smooth curved surfaces, add detail to terrain, or enhance the appearance of characters.

Tessellation shaders control the subdivision process, generating new vertices and normals to create a more refined mesh.

7. Shader Graph Tools

For those who prefer a more visual approach to shader development, shader graph tools like Shader Graph in Unity or Unreal Engine's Material Editor provide a node-based interface for creating and connecting shader nodes. These tools can simplify the process of building complex shaders and experimenting with different effects.

Implementing Advanced Shading

Implementing these advanced shading techniques requires a deeper understanding of lighting, material properties, and shader programming. However, the results can be truly impressive, elevating the visual realism and artistic expression of your Vulkan applications.

By exploring and incorporating these advanced shading techniques, you can push the boundaries of visual fidelity and create stunningly realistic and immersive 3D experiences.

Part III: Advanced Vulkan Development

Chapter 9: Performance Optimization

Profiling and Benchmarking Your Applications

As a tech expert with over 20 years of experience, you know that creating visually impressive graphics is only half the battle. Ensuring your Vulkan applications perform smoothly and efficiently is equally crucial, especially when targeting demanding platforms or resource-constrained devices. Profiling and benchmarking are indispensable tools in your arsenal, providing the insights needed to identify bottlenecks and optimize your applications for peak performance.

Profiling: Unveiling Performance Bottlenecks

Profiling involves analyzing your application's execution to identify performance hotspots – areas where the application spends a significant amount of time or resources. By pinpointing these bottlenecks, you can focus your optimization efforts on the areas that will yield the greatest improvements.

Vulkan Profiling Layers

The Vulkan SDK provides profiling layers that can capture a wealth of performance data, including:

- **Function Timing:** Measures the time spent in various Vulkan functions and API calls.
- **GPU Timings:** Records the time taken by different GPU operations, such as draw calls, compute dispatches, and memory transfers.
- **Pipeline Statistics:** Gathers statistics about pipeline state changes, shader invocations, and primitive counts.
- **Memory Usage:** Tracks memory allocations and usage patterns.

By enabling these profiling layers, you can gain valuable insights into the performance characteristics of your application.

Profiling Tools

Several tools can visualize and analyze the data collected by the Vulkan profiling layers:

- **Vulkan Profiler:** A standalone tool included in the Vulkan SDK that provides a graphical interface for visualizing and analyzing profiling data.
- **RenderDoc:** A powerful graphics debugger that also includes profiling capabilities, allowing you to correlate performance data with specific frames and draw calls.

- **GPU Vendor Profilers:** GPU vendors like NVIDIA, AMD, and Intel offer their own profiling tools that provide detailed insights into GPU performance and resource utilization.

Benchmarking: Measuring Performance

Benchmarking involves running your application under controlled conditions and measuring its performance metrics, such as frame rate, CPU utilization, and GPU usage. This allows you to:

- **Establish a Baseline:** Measure the initial performance of your application before applying any optimizations.
- **Evaluate Optimizations:** Quantify the impact of your optimizations by comparing benchmark results before and after the changes.
- **Compare Performance:** Compare the performance of your application on different hardware configurations or against other rendering APIs.

Designing Benchmarks

When designing benchmarks, consider the following:

- **Representative Workloads:** Choose workloads that accurately reflect the typical usage of your application.

- **Consistent Conditions:** Ensure that the benchmarking environment and parameters remain consistent across different runs.
- **Meaningful Metrics:** Select performance metrics that are relevant to your application and goals.
- **Statistical Significance:** Run the benchmark multiple times and average the results to reduce variability and ensure statistical significance.

Performance Optimization Strategies

Once you've identified performance bottlenecks through profiling and benchmarking, you can apply various optimization strategies:

- **Reduce Draw Calls:** Batch geometry, use instancing, and minimize state changes to reduce the number of draw calls.
- **Optimize Shaders:** Simplify shader code, reduce memory accesses, and utilize built-in functions to improve shader efficiency.
- **Efficient Memory Management:** Use appropriate memory types, minimize memory transfers, and utilize staging buffers for optimal data transfer.
- **Texture Optimization:** Use appropriate texture formats, mipmapping, and anisotropic filtering to optimize texture usage.

- **Pipeline Optimization:** Create pipeline state objects (PSOs) upfront to reduce pipeline creation overhead.
- **Concurrency:** Utilize multi-threading and asynchronous compute to parallelize tasks and maximize GPU utilization.

Continuous Optimization

Performance optimization is an ongoing process. As your application evolves, new bottlenecks may emerge, requiring further analysis and optimization. Regularly profile and benchmark your application to identify and address performance issues, ensuring that your Vulkan applications run smoothly and efficiently.

Reducing Draw Calls and Batching

As you delve deeper into Vulkan optimization, you'll discover that minimizing draw calls is a key strategy for enhancing rendering performance. Each draw call incurs CPU overhead as it involves communication between the CPU and GPU. By reducing the number of draw calls, you can free up CPU cycles, allowing for smoother frame rates and improved overall efficiency.

Understanding Draw Calls

A draw call essentially instructs the GPU to render a set of primitives using a specific pipeline state and a set of resources. Factors that contribute to draw call overhead include:

- **Pipeline State Changes:** Switching between different pipelines (shaders, blend modes, etc.) requires the GPU to reconfigure its internal state, incurring a cost.
- **Resource Binding:** Binding buffers and textures to the pipeline involves communication between the CPU and GPU.
- **Command Buffer Submission:** Submitting command buffers to the GPU queues also adds overhead.

Batching: Combining Draw Calls

Batching is a powerful technique that combines multiple draw calls into a single, larger draw call. This reduces the overall number of draw calls and minimizes the associated overhead. There are different approaches to batching:

1. Static Batching:

Static batching combines the geometry of multiple static objects (those that don't move or change) into a single, larger vertex buffer. This allows you to render all the objects with a single draw call, significantly reducing CPU overhead.

2. Dynamic Batching:

Dynamic batching combines the geometry of multiple dynamic objects (those that move or change) into a single draw call. This is more challenging than static batching, as the combined geometry needs to be updated each frame. However, it can still provide significant performance improvements for scenes with many moving objects.

3. Instancing:

Instancing, as discussed earlier, allows you to render multiple instances of the same object with a single draw call. This is particularly effective for rendering large numbers of similar objects, such as trees, grass, or particles.

Implementing Batching in Vulkan

To implement batching in Vulkan, you need to:

- **Identify Batchable Objects:** Group objects that share the same material and rendering state.
- **Combine Geometry:** Combine the vertex data of the batched objects into a single vertex buffer.

- **Adjust Indices:** If using index buffers, adjust the indices to reference the combined vertex buffer.
- **Issue a Single Draw Call:** Render the combined geometry with a single draw call.

Challenges and Considerations

- **State Changes:** Batching is most effective when objects share the same rendering state. If objects have different materials or require different pipeline states, batching might not be beneficial.
- **Transformations:** When batching dynamic objects, you need to update the transformation matrices for each object in the combined vertex buffer each frame.
- **Batch Size:** The optimal batch size depends on various factors, such as the complexity of the geometry and the hardware capabilities. Experiment to find the best balance between reducing draw calls and avoiding excessively large batches.

Benefits of Reducing Draw Calls

- **Improved CPU Performance:** Frees up CPU cycles, allowing for smoother frame rates and improved responsiveness.
- **Reduced Overhead:** Minimizes the overhead associated with pipeline state changes, resource binding, and command buffer submission.

- **Increased Rendering Throughput:** Allows the GPU to render more objects in the same amount of time.

By understanding the impact of draw calls and utilizing batching techniques effectively, you can significantly optimize the rendering performance of your Vulkan applications, especially in scenes with large numbers of objects. This leads to smoother frame rates, improved responsiveness, and a more enjoyable user experience.

Optimizing Shader Code

As an experienced tech expert, you know that shaders are the heart of your graphics pipeline, responsible for transforming and coloring the pixels that bring your 3D scenes to life. However, inefficient shader code can significantly impact rendering performance. Let's explore techniques to optimize your shader code and squeeze every ounce of performance from your Vulkan applications.

1. Understanding Shader Execution

Before diving into optimization, it's crucial to understand how shaders are executed on the GPU. GPUs excel at parallel processing, executing the same shader code on multiple data elements (vertices or fragments) simultaneously. However, certain coding practices can hinder this parallelism and lead to performance bottlenecks.

2. Common Shader Bottlenecks

- **Complex Calculations:** Avoid unnecessary or overly complex mathematical operations that consume significant processing time.
- **Redundant Calculations:** Identify and eliminate redundant calculations by storing intermediate results in variables.
- **Excessive Memory Access:** Minimize accesses to memory, especially global memory, as it can be a major performance bottleneck. Utilize local variables and registers to store frequently accessed data.
- **Branching:** Branching (if-else statements) can disrupt the parallel execution of shaders, as different threads might take different branches. Minimize branching or use techniques like predication to avoid it.
- **Loop Unrolling:** For small loops with a fixed number of iterations, consider unrolling them to reduce loop overhead. However, be mindful of the potential increase in code size.
- **Function Calls:** Function calls can introduce overhead. Inline small functions or consider alternatives if possible.

3. Optimization Techniques

- **Simplify Expressions:** Simplify mathematical expressions and use built-in functions optimized for the hardware.
- **Use Constants:** Declare frequently used values as constants to avoid redundant calculations.
- **Optimize Memory Layout:** Organize data structures in a way that minimizes memory access and improves cache utilization.
- **Vectorize Operations:** Utilize vector operations to perform calculations on multiple data elements simultaneously.
- **Reduce Precision:** Use lower precision data types (e.g., half instead of float) when possible to reduce memory bandwidth and computation.
- **Early Exits:** Use early exits in shaders to avoid unnecessary calculations for fragments that will be discarded.

4. Shader Specialization

Vulkan offers shader specialization, which allows you to customize shader code at compile time with constant values. This can help optimize shaders for specific scenarios or hardware configurations.

5. Tools for Shader Optimization

- **Shader Compilers:** Modern shader compilers often perform optimizations automatically. Explore compiler options to enable different optimization levels.
- **Profiling Tools:** Use profiling tools to identify performance hotspots in your shaders and guide your optimization efforts.
- **Disassemblers:** Examine the disassembled shader code to understand how the compiler translates your code and identify potential areas for improvement.

6. Best Practices

- **Write Clean Code:** Well-structured and commented code is easier to understand and optimize.
- **Profile Regularly:** Profile your shaders to identify bottlenecks and track the impact of your optimizations.
- **Test Thoroughly:** Ensure that your optimizations do not introduce visual artifacts or regressions.
- **Stay Updated:** Keep up with the latest shader optimization techniques and best practices.

By applying these optimization techniques and utilizing the available tools, you can fine-tune your shader code for peak performance, ensuring that your Vulkan applications deliver stunning visuals without compromising efficiency.

Memory Management Best Practices

As an experienced tech expert, you understand that efficient memory management is crucial for achieving optimal performance in Vulkan applications. Vulkan provides explicit control over memory allocation, offering the flexibility to fine-tune memory usage for your specific needs. Let's explore some best practices to maximize efficiency and avoid common pitfalls.

1. Understanding Vulkan's Memory Model

Vulkan's memory model distinguishes between host memory (accessible by the CPU) and device memory (residing on the GPU). Each physical device has memory heaps with different characteristics, and within each heap, there are memory types with specific properties (host visible, host coherent, device local, etc.).

2. Choosing the Right Memory Type

Selecting the appropriate memory type for your resources is crucial:

- **Device Local:** Prioritize device-local memory for resources that are frequently accessed by the

GPU (e.g., textures, vertex buffers). This minimizes data transfer overhead.

- **Host Visible/Coherent:** Use host-visible and coherent memory for resources that need to be accessed by both the CPU and GPU (e.g., uniform buffers that are frequently updated).
- **Staging Buffers:** For large data transfers, utilize staging buffers in host-visible memory to transfer data to device-local memory efficiently.

3. Memory Allocation

- **Vulkan Memory Allocator (VMA):** Consider using VMA, a library that simplifies memory allocation and management in Vulkan. VMA provides efficient allocation strategies and helps avoid memory fragmentation.
- **Dedicated Allocations:** For large resources, prefer dedicated memory allocations to avoid fragmentation and improve performance.
- **Sparse Memory:** For very large resources, explore using sparse memory, which allows you to allocate and use large memory regions without committing all the physical memory upfront.

4. Memory Mapping

- **Minimize Mapping:** Avoid frequent mapping and unmapping of device memory, as it can introduce synchronization overhead.

- **Persistent Mapping:** If possible, map memory persistently and update it directly instead of repeatedly mapping and unmapping.

5. Resource Reuse

- **Buffer and Image Sub-allocation:** Divide larger buffers or images into smaller sub-allocations to reuse memory efficiently.
- **Recycling:** Recycle and reuse memory for temporary or short-lived resources.

6. Memory Aliasing

- **Multiple Bindings:** Utilize memory aliasing to bind the same memory to different resources, enabling different views of the same data.

7. Synchronization

- **Proper Barriers:** Use memory barriers and synchronization primitives (semaphores, fences) to ensure correct access and prevent data races when sharing resources between the CPU and GPU or between different queues.

8. Monitoring Memory Usage

- **Debugging Tools:** Utilize debugging tools and validation layers to identify memory leaks or incorrect usage.

- **Profiling:** Profile your application to monitor memory usage patterns and identify potential areas for optimization.

9. Best Practices

- **Plan Ahead:** Plan your memory usage strategy early in development to avoid costly refactoring later.
- **Minimize Allocations:** Reduce the number of memory allocations by reusing and recycling resources.
- **Avoid Fragmentation:** Choose appropriate allocation strategies to prevent memory fragmentation.
- **Optimize Data Transfers:** Utilize staging buffers and efficient transfer techniques for large data transfers.

By following these best practices and carefully managing memory usage in your Vulkan applications, you can ensure optimal performance, reduce memory footprint, and avoid common memory-related issues. This leads to smoother frame rates, improved stability, and a more enjoyable user experience.

Chapter 10: Compute Shaders

Introduction to General-Purpose GPU Programming

As a seasoned tech expert, you've witnessed the evolution of GPUs from specialized graphics processors to highly parallel computing powerhouses. While their primary function remains graphics rendering, their parallel architecture lends itself well to a broader range of applications. This is where general-purpose GPU (GPGPU) programming comes in, allowing you to harness the massive computational power of GPUs for tasks beyond traditional graphics.

The Rise of GPGPU

Historically, GPUs were designed solely for accelerating graphics rendering. However, as their processing power increased, developers recognized their potential for general-purpose computation. GPGPU programming emerged as a way to leverage this power for tasks such as:

- **Scientific Computing:** Simulations, physics calculations, climate modeling
- **Image and Video Processing:** Filtering, enhancement, object recognition

- **Machine Learning:** Training neural networks, deep learning
- **Financial Modeling:** Risk analysis, option pricing
- **Cryptography:** Hashing, encryption, decryption

The Advantages of GPGPU

GPUs offer several advantages for general-purpose computation:

- **Massive Parallelism:** GPUs possess thousands of cores designed for parallel execution, enabling them to handle massive datasets and perform computations concurrently.
- **High Memory Bandwidth:** GPUs have dedicated high-bandwidth memory, allowing for rapid data access and transfer.
- **Increased Computational Throughput:** For parallelizable tasks, GPUs can significantly outperform CPUs in terms of computational throughput.
- **Cost-Effectiveness:** Leveraging existing GPUs for general-purpose computation can be more cost-effective than investing in specialized hardware.

Compute Shaders: The Workhorse of GPGPU

Compute shaders are specialized programs that run on the GPU and perform general-purpose computations. They operate independently of the graphics rendering pipeline, allowing you to execute parallel computations on arbitrary data.

Key Concepts in GPGPU Programming

- **Parallel Execution:** GPGPU programming requires a different mindset than traditional CPU programming. You need to design your algorithms to exploit the parallel architecture of the GPU.
- **Data Parallelism:** Divide your data into smaller chunks that can be processed concurrently by multiple GPU cores.
- **Memory Management:** Efficiently manage data transfer between the CPU and GPU and utilize different memory spaces (global, shared, constant) effectively.
- **Synchronization:** Synchronize threads and ensure data consistency when multiple threads access shared data.

Vulkan and Compute Shaders

Vulkan provides excellent support for GPGPU programming through compute shaders. You can:

- **Create Compute Pipelines:** Define compute pipelines that encapsulate the compute shader and its execution parameters.
- **Dispatch Compute Work:** Dispatch compute work items to the GPU, specifying the number of workgroups and work items per group.
- **Access Memory:** Access various memory spaces (global, shared, constant) within your compute shaders.
- **Synchronize Threads:** Use synchronization primitives (barriers) to coordinate access to shared data and ensure correct execution order.

GPGPU Libraries and Frameworks

Several libraries and frameworks simplify GPGPU programming:

- **OpenCL:** An open standard for cross-platform parallel programming on heterogeneous devices (CPUs, GPUs, FPGAs).
- **CUDA:** A parallel computing platform and API developed by NVIDIA for their GPUs.
- **Vulkan Kompute:** A framework that simplifies the use of Vulkan compute shaders.

Applications of GPGPU

GPGPU programming has a wide range of applications:

- **Physics Simulations:** Simulate cloth, fluids, rigid bodies, and other physical phenomena.
- **Image Processing:** Apply filters, enhance images, perform object recognition.
- **Machine Learning:** Train and execute neural networks for various tasks.
- **Scientific Computing:** Perform complex calculations and simulations in fields like physics, chemistry, and biology.

By understanding the principles of GPGPU programming and utilizing Vulkan's compute capabilities, you can unlock the vast potential of GPUs for general-purpose computation, accelerating a wide range of applications and pushing the boundaries of what's possible with parallel processing.

Compute Pipeline and Dispatching

As an experienced tech expert, you know that compute shaders, the heart of general-purpose GPU programming, require a specialized pipeline to execute efficiently. In Vulkan, the compute pipeline encapsulates the compute shader and its associated state, providing a streamlined path for dispatching and executing compute workloads on the GPU.

Creating a Compute Pipeline

Creating a compute pipeline in Vulkan involves the following steps:

1. **Create a Shader Module:** First, create a shader module that contains the compiled SPIR-V code of your compute shader.
2. **Specify Pipeline Layout:** Define a pipeline layout that specifies any descriptor sets or push constants used by the compute shader.
3. **Populate** VkComputePipelineCreateInfo**:** Fill in a VkComputePipelineCreateInfo structure with the shader module, pipeline layout, and any other relevant state information.
4. **Create the Pipeline:** Call the vkCreateComputePipelines function to create the compute pipeline object.

Dispatching Compute Work

Once you have a compute pipeline, you can dispatch compute work to the GPU. This involves dividing your workload into smaller units called workgroups, which are further divided into individual work items.

1. **Determine Workgroup Size:** Specify the number of work items in each workgroup based on the nature of your computation and the hardware capabilities.

2. **Calculate Dispatch Dimensions:** Calculate the number of workgroups needed to cover your entire workload.
3. **Bind Pipeline and Dispatch:** Bind the compute pipeline to the command buffer and use the vkCmdDispatch function to dispatch the compute work, specifying the number of workgroups in each dimension (X, Y, Z).

Workgroups and Work Items

- **Workgroups:** Groups of work items that execute concurrently on the GPU. They can share data through shared memory and synchronize their execution using barriers.
- **Work Items:** Individual threads of execution within a workgroup. Each work item has a unique ID that can be used to access and process specific data elements.

Synchronization

Synchronization is crucial in compute shaders to ensure correct execution when multiple work items access shared data. Vulkan provides barriers that allow you to synchronize memory access and execution within and between workgroups.

Code Example: Dispatching Compute Work

```cpp
C++

// ... Create compute pipeline ...


// Bind compute pipeline

vkCmdBindPipeline(commandBuffer,
VK_PIPELINE_BIND_POINT_COMPUTE,
computePipeline);


// Dispatch compute work

vkCmdDispatch(commandBuffer,      workgroupCountX,
workgroupCountY, workgroupCountZ);
```

Benefits of Compute Pipelines

- **Encapsulation:** Encapsulates the compute shader and its associated state, improving code organization and maintainability.
- **Efficiency:** Allows the driver to perform optimizations and reduce pipeline creation overhead.
- **Flexibility:** Provides flexibility in configuring the compute pipeline for different workloads and hardware.

Compute Shaders vs. Graphics Pipeline

While compute shaders operate independently of the graphics pipeline, they share some similarities:

- **Shader Stages:** Both utilize shader stages for processing data.
- **Pipeline Objects:** Both use pipeline objects to encapsulate shader code and state.
- **Resource Binding:** Both can access resources like buffers and images through descriptor sets.

However, there are key differences:

- **Execution Model:** Compute shaders operate on a grid of workgroups and work items, while the graphics pipeline processes vertices and fragments.
- **Output:** Compute shaders typically output data to buffers or images, while the graphics pipeline outputs rendered images.

By understanding the concepts of compute pipelines and dispatching, you can effectively harness the parallel processing power of GPUs for general-purpose computation, accelerating a wide range of applications and pushing the boundaries of what's possible with Vulkan.

Shared Memory and Synchronization

As an experienced tech expert, you know that efficient parallel execution on the GPU often requires coordination and communication between work items within a workgroup. Shared memory and synchronization primitives provide the mechanisms for achieving this coordination, enabling powerful parallel algorithms and efficient data sharing.

Shared Memory: A Collaborative Workspace

Shared memory is a limited but high-speed memory region that is accessible to all work items within a workgroup. It acts as a collaborative workspace where work items can exchange data and cooperate on computations.

Benefits of Shared Memory:

- **High Speed:** Shared memory is significantly faster than global memory, enabling rapid data exchange within a workgroup.
- **Reduced Global Memory Access:** By caching frequently accessed data in shared memory, you can reduce costly accesses to global memory.
- **Collaboration:** Facilitates collaborative algorithms where work items share intermediate results or cooperate on computations.

Synchronization: Ensuring Data Consistency

Synchronization is crucial when multiple work items access shared memory concurrently. Without proper synchronization, data races can occur, leading to unpredictable and incorrect results.

Vulkan provides synchronization primitives, primarily barriers, to coordinate memory access and execution within a workgroup.

Types of Barriers:

- **Memory Barriers:** Ensure that memory operations are performed in the correct order, preventing data hazards.
- **Execution Barriers:** Synchronize the execution of work items within a workgroup, ensuring that all work items reach a certain point before proceeding.

Using Shared Memory and Synchronization

To utilize shared memory and synchronization in your compute shaders:

1. **Declare Shared Memory:** Declare shared variables within your compute shader using the shared keyword.
2. **Populate Shared Memory:** Load data from global memory into shared memory.

3. **Synchronize Access:** Use barriers to synchronize access to shared memory and ensure that all work items have a consistent view of the data.
4. **Perform Computations:** Perform computations using the data in shared memory.
5. **Write Back (Optional):** Write results back to global memory if necessary.

Code Example: Shared Memory and Synchronization

OpenGL Shading Language

```
#version 450

layout(local_size_x = 16) in; // Workgroup size

shared vec4 sharedData[16];

void main() {
    // Load data into shared memory
        sharedData[gl_LocalInvocationID.x]      =
data[gl_GlobalInvocationID.x];
```

```
// Synchronize work items

barrier();


// Perform computations using sharedData

// ...


// Synchronize before writing back (if necessary)

barrier();


// Write results back to global memory (optional)

// ...

}
```

Best Practices

- **Minimize Synchronization:** Excessive use of barriers can hinder performance. Strive to minimize synchronization overhead.
- **Optimize Memory Access Patterns:** Access shared memory in a coalesced manner to maximize memory bandwidth utilization.

- **Consider Workgroup Size:** Choose a workgroup size that balances shared memory usage and occupancy (the number of active workgroups on the GPU).

Shared Memory and Synchronization in Action

Shared memory and synchronization are essential for implementing efficient parallel algorithms on the GPU. They are used in various applications, including:

- **Reduction Operations:** Efficiently calculate sums, averages, or other aggregate values across a large dataset.
- **Image Filtering:** Apply filters to images by sharing data between neighboring pixels.
- **Sorting and Searching:** Implement parallel sorting and searching algorithms.

By understanding the concepts of shared memory and synchronization, you can unlock the full potential of Vulkan compute shaders for general-purpose GPU programming. This enables you to implement complex parallel algorithms, optimize data sharing, and achieve significant performance gains in your applications.

Example: Particle System with Compute Shaders

Particle systems are a staple of real-time graphics, used to simulate a wide range of effects, from smoke and fire to explosions and magic spells. Compute shaders provide an ideal mechanism for implementing particle systems, leveraging the parallel processing power of the GPU to efficiently update and render vast numbers of particles.

Particle System Structure

A typical particle system consists of the following components:

- **Particles:** The individual particles that make up the system, each with properties like position, velocity, color, and lifetime.
- **Emitter:** The source of the particles, defining their initial properties and spawning behavior.
- **Updater:** The logic that updates the particles' properties over time, such as applying forces, simulating collisions, and fading colors.
- **Renderer:** The component that renders the particles to the screen, typically using point sprites or other simple geometry.

Compute Shader Implementation

In a compute shader-based particle system, the updater is implemented as a compute shader. This shader operates on a buffer of particle data, updating each particle's properties in parallel.

1. **Particle Data:** Store the particle data in a storage buffer, allowing the compute shader to read and write particle properties.
2. **Emitter:** Initialize the particle data with initial properties based on the emitter's settings.
3. **Updater (Compute Shader):**
   - Access the particle data buffer.
   - For each particle:
     - Update its position based on velocity.
     - Apply forces (gravity, wind, etc.).
     - Simulate collisions (optional).
     - Update color and other properties.
     - Decrease lifetime.
     - If lifetime reaches zero, re-spawn the particle.
4. **Renderer:** Render the particles using the updated data, typically using instanced rendering with point sprites.

Code Example (Simplified)

OpenGL Shading Language

```glsl
#version 450

layout(local_size_x = 64) in;

struct Particle {
  vec3 position;
  vec3 velocity;
  vec4 color;
  float lifetime;
};

layout(binding = 0) buffer ParticleBuffer {
  Particle particles[];
};

void main() {
  uint index = gl_GlobalInvocationID.x;
  Particle particle = particles[index];
```

```
// Update position

particle.position += particle.velocity * deltaTime;


// Apply gravity

particle.velocity += vec3(0.0, -9.8, 0.0) * deltaTime;


// ... other updates ...


// Decrease lifetime

particle.lifetime -= deltaTime;


// Respawn if necessary

if (particle.lifetime <= 0.0) {

  // ... initialize with new properties ...

}


// Store updated particle
```

```
particles[index] = particle;

}
```

Benefits of Compute Shaders

- **Efficiency:** Leverages the parallel processing power of the GPU for efficient particle updates.
- **Flexibility:** Allows for complex particle behavior and interactions.
- **Integration:** Seamlessly integrates with Vulkan's rendering pipeline.

Advanced Features

- **Collisions:** Implement collision detection and response using techniques like spatial partitioning or collision shaders.
- **Sorted Particles:** Sort particles based on depth for correct alpha blending.
- **Particle Interactions:** Simulate interactions between particles, such as attraction or repulsion.

By utilizing compute shaders for particle systems, you can create stunning visual effects with thousands or even millions of particles, adding a dynamic and immersive element to your Vulkan applications.

Chapter 11: Advanced Rendering Techniques

Deferred Shading

As a seasoned tech expert, you're familiar with the traditional forward rendering approach, where each object is rendered and lit individually. While straightforward, this method becomes inefficient in complex scenes with numerous lights, as each object needs to be processed for every light source. Deferred shading offers an alternative approach that decouples geometry processing from lighting calculations, enabling efficient rendering of scenes with a large number of lights.[1]

The Two-Pass Approach

Deferred shading involves two main passes:[2]

1. **Geometry Pass:**
   - Render the scene once, capturing geometric information (position, normal, color, etc.) into a set of textures called the G-buffer.[3]
   - No lighting calculations are performed in this pass.
2. **Lighting Pass:**

- Use the G-buffer information to perform lighting calculations for each pixel on the screen.[4]
- Light sources are processed individually, and their contributions are accumulated for each pixel.[5]

The G-Buffer: A Repository of Geometric Information

The G-buffer typically consists of multiple textures, each storing a different aspect of the scene's geometry:[6]

- **Position:** Stores the world-space position of each pixel.
- **Normal:** Stores the world-space normal vector of each pixel.[7]
- **Color:** Stores the diffuse color or albedo of each pixel.[8]
- **Other Attributes:** May include specular color, roughness, metallic properties, or other material attributes.[9]

Benefits of Deferred Shading

- **Efficiency with Many Lights:** Handles a large number of lights efficiently, as lighting calculations are performed only once per pixel, regardless of the number of lights.

- **Decoupled Geometry and Lighting:** Allows for more complex lighting models and effects, as lighting is handled separately from geometry processing.[10]
- **Flexibility:** Enables various post-processing effects and optimizations, as the G-buffer provides access to geometric information for each pixel.[11]

Challenges of Deferred Shading

- **Increased Memory Usage:** Requires additional memory to store the G-buffer textures.
- **Transparency Handling:** Traditional deferred shading struggles with transparency, requiring specialized techniques or forward rendering for transparent objects.[12]
- **Bandwidth Requirements:** Accessing the G-buffer textures can increase memory bandwidth usage.

Implementing Deferred Shading in Vulkan

1. **Geometry Pass:**
   - Create a render pass with multiple color attachments for the G-buffer textures.
   - Render the scene, outputting the desired geometric attributes to the corresponding attachments.
2. **Lighting Pass:**

- Create a separate render pass that uses the G-buffer textures as input attachments.
- Use a full-screen quad to process each pixel on the screen.[13]
- For each light source:
  - Calculate the light's contribution to each pixel based on the G-buffer information.[14]
  - Accumulate the light contributions.
- Output the final color to the screen.

Code Example (Simplified)

OpenGL Shading Language

```
// Geometry pass fragment shader

layout(location = 0) out vec4 gPosition;

layout(location = 1) out vec3 gNormal;

layout(location = 2) out vec4 gAlbedo;


void main() {

    // ... calculate and output position, normal, and albedo
    ...

}
```

```glsl
// Lighting pass fragment shader

layout(input_attachment_index = 0) uniform
subpassInput gPosition;

layout(input_attachment_index = 1) uniform
subpassInput gNormal;

layout(input_attachment_index = 2) uniform
subpassInput gAlbedo;


void main() {

    vec3 position = subpassLoad(gPosition).xyz;

    vec3 normal = subpassLoad(gNormal).xyz;

    vec4 albedo = subpassLoad(gAlbedo);


    // ... perform lighting calculations ...

}
```

Optimizations

- **Light Culling:** Cull lights that don't affect the current pixel to reduce lighting calculations.[15]
- **Tiled Deferred Shading:** Divide the screen into tiles and process lights per tile to improve cache coherency.
- **Clustered Deferred Shading:** Group lights into clusters to reduce the number of lights processed per pixel.

Deferred Shading in Action

Deferred shading is widely used in modern game engines and 3D applications to efficiently render scenes with complex lighting and numerous light sources.[16] It enables realistic and immersive environments with dynamic lighting effects, pushing the boundaries of visual fidelity.

By understanding the principles and implementation of deferred shading, you can add a powerful rendering technique to your Vulkan toolkit, enabling you to create visually stunning and performant 3D applications.

Tessellation

Tessellation is an advanced rendering technique that allows you to dynamically subdivide polygons into smaller primitives, effectively increasing the geometric detail of your models. This technique is particularly useful for creating smooth curved surfaces from simpler base shapes, adding detail to terrain, or enhancing the appearance of characters and objects.

The Tessellation Pipeline

Tessellation is integrated into the Vulkan rendering pipeline as an optional stage that occurs after vertex shading but before geometry shading. It involves three main steps:

1. **Tessellation Control Shader (TCS):**
   - Determines the tessellation level, which controls how much the input patch (a group of vertices defining a surface) is subdivided.
   - Can also perform per-patch calculations and modify vertex attributes.
2. **Tessellation Primitive Generator (Fixed-Function):**
   - Subdivides the input patch based on the tessellation levels specified by the TCS.
   - Generates new vertices and connects them to form smaller primitives.
3. **Tessellation Evaluation Shader (TES):**
   - Calculates the positions and other attributes of the newly generated vertices.
   - Can also perform per-vertex calculations and modify attributes.

Tessellation Levels

The tessellation level controls the degree of subdivision. Higher tessellation levels result in more detailed geometry, while lower levels produce coarser representations. Tessellation levels can be specified per edge or per patch, allowing for adaptive tessellation based on factors like distance from the viewer or surface curvature.

Benefits of Tessellation

- **Dynamic Level of Detail:** Adjust the level of detail based on viewing distance or other criteria, optimizing performance and visual quality.
- **Smooth Curved Surfaces:** Create smooth curved surfaces from simpler base shapes, reducing the need for high-resolution models.
- **Efficient Geometry:** Represent complex geometry with fewer base primitives, reducing memory usage and potentially improving performance.

Implementing Tessellation in Vulkan

1. **Enable Tessellation in Pipeline:** During pipeline creation, enable tessellation by setting the VkPipelineTessellationStateCreateInfo structure's patchControlPoints member to the number of control points per patch.

2. **Create Tessellation Shaders:** Write tessellation control and evaluation shaders in GLSL and compile them into SPIR-V modules.
3. **Specify Tessellation State:** Configure the tessellation state in the VkGraphicsPipelineCreateInfo structure, including the tessellation shaders and other relevant parameters.

Code Example (Simplified)

C++

```
// ... Enable tessellation in pipeline creation ...


// Create tessellation shaders

VkShaderModule         tescShaderModule         =
createShaderModule(device, tescShaderCode);

VkShaderModule         teseShaderModule         =
createShaderModule(device, teseShaderCode);


// ... Specify tessellation state in pipeline creation ...
```

Applications of Tessellation

- **Terrain Rendering:** Create realistic terrain with varying levels of detail based on distance.
- **Character Modeling:** Smooth out character models and add detail to features like hair or clothing.
- **Displacement Mapping:** Displace vertices based on a displacement map to create detailed surfaces.
- **Organic Modeling:** Generate organic shapes and structures with smooth curves and intricate details.

Tessellation and Performance

While tessellation can enhance visual fidelity, it's important to consider its performance implications. Higher tessellation levels increase the number of primitives to process, potentially impacting rendering performance. Utilize techniques like level-of-detail control and adaptive tessellation to balance visual quality with performance efficiency.

By understanding the principles and implementation of tessellation, you can add a powerful tool to your Vulkan rendering arsenal. This technique allows you to dynamically adjust the level of detail in your scenes, creating smooth curved surfaces, and enhancing the visual appeal of your applications.

Geometry Shaders

As an experienced tech expert, you understand the limitations of the vertex shader, which operates on individual vertices, and the tessellation stage, which focuses on subdividing existing primitives. Geometry shaders offer a powerful tool to bridge this gap, allowing you to operate on entire primitives, creating new primitives, or modifying existing ones. This unlocks a wide range of effects and rendering techniques that would be challenging or impossible to achieve with other shader stages.

The Role of Geometry Shaders

Geometry shaders sit within the Vulkan rendering pipeline between the tessellation stage and the rasterization stage. They receive complete primitives as input, such as points, lines, or triangles, and have the capability to:

- **Expand Primitives:** Generate multiple output primitives from a single input primitive. This is useful for effects like fur rendering, where each vertex can generate multiple fur strands.
- **Modify Primitives:** Alter the type or properties of existing primitives. For example, convert a line into a triangle strip or adjust the positions of vertices.

- **Discard Primitives:** Cull primitives based on certain criteria, optimizing rendering by discarding unnecessary geometry.
- **Emit Data:** Output data to transform feedback buffers, which can be used for particle physics or other computations.

Input and Output

Geometry shaders receive input in the form of an array of vertices that define the input primitive. The size of this array depends on the type of primitive. For example, a triangle input will provide an array of three vertices.

The output of a geometry shader is a stream of primitives, which can be of a different type than the input primitive. For example, a geometry shader could receive a point as input and output a triangle strip.

Implementing Geometry Shaders in Vulkan

1. **Enable Geometry Shaders in Pipeline:** During pipeline creation, enable geometry shaders by providing a VkPipelineShaderStageCreateInfo structure for the geometry shader stage.
2. **Write Geometry Shader:** Write your geometry shader in GLSL, specifying the input primitive type, output primitive type, and maximum number of vertices to be emitted.

3. **Compile and Link:** Compile your geometry shader into a SPIR-V module and link it with the other shader stages in your pipeline.

Code Example (Simplified)

OpenGL Shading Language

```
#version 450

layout(triangles) in;
layout(triangle_strip, max_vertices = 4) out;

void main() {
    // ... process input triangle ...


    // Emit new vertices to form a quad
    gl_Position = ...;
    EmitVertex();


    gl_Position = ...;
```

```
EmitVertex();


gl_Position = ...;

EmitVertex();


gl_Position = ...;

EmitVertex();


EndPrimitive();

}
```

Applications of Geometry Shaders

- **Fur and Hair Rendering:** Generate multiple fur strands or hair strands from each vertex.
- **Shadow Volume Extrusion:** Extrude shadow volumes from objects to create realistic shadows.
- **Particle Systems:** Generate particles with varying properties and behaviors.
- **Silhouette Extraction:** Detect and highlight the silhouette edges of objects.

- **Procedural Geometry:** Create complex geometric shapes and patterns procedurally.

Geometry Shaders and Performance

While geometry shaders offer powerful capabilities, they can also introduce performance overhead. Consider the following:

- **Increased Processing:** Processing entire primitives can be more computationally expensive than processing individual vertices.
- **Memory Access:** Accessing and modifying multiple vertices within a primitive can increase memory traffic.
- **Output Limitations:** The maximum number of vertices that can be emitted by a geometry shader is limited by the hardware.

Balancing Flexibility and Performance

When utilizing geometry shaders, it's crucial to balance their flexibility with performance considerations. Carefully analyze your use case and optimize your shader code to minimize overhead and maximize efficiency.

By understanding the capabilities and limitations of geometry shaders, you can leverage their power to create a wide range of advanced rendering effects and expand the geometric possibilities in your Vulkan applications.

Screen-Space Ambient Occlusion (SSAO)

As an experienced tech expert, you understand the importance of subtle details in creating realistic and immersive 3D scenes. Ambient occlusion (AO) is a shading technique that simulates the soft shadows that occur in crevices and corners where ambient light is blocked or occluded. Screen-space ambient occlusion (SSAO) is a popular and efficient technique for approximating AO in real-time, adding depth and realism to your Vulkan applications.

The Concept of Ambient Occlusion

Ambient occlusion simulates the self-shadowing that occurs when ambient light is blocked by nearby geometry. Areas that are surrounded by more geometry, such as corners or crevices, receive less ambient light and appear darker, while areas that are more exposed receive more ambient light and appear brighter. This subtle shading effect enhances the perception of depth and contact between objects in the scene.

SSAO: An Approximation in Screen Space

SSAO approximates ambient occlusion by analyzing the depth buffer in screen space. For each pixel on the screen, it samples the depth values of neighboring pixels and calculates an occlusion factor based on the geometric complexity in the neighborhood. This occlusion factor is then used to darken the pixel's color, simulating the effect of ambient occlusion.

Implementation Steps

1. **Generate Sample Points:** Generate a set of random sample points in a hemisphere around the current pixel.
2. **Sample Depth Buffer:** For each sample point, project it into screen space and sample the depth buffer at the projected location.
3. **Calculate Occlusion:** Compare the sampled depth with the depth of the current pixel. If the sampled depth is closer to the camera, it contributes to the occlusion factor.
4. **Accumulate Occlusion:** Accumulate the occlusion contributions from all sample points.
5. **Apply Occlusion:** Multiply the pixel's color by the calculated occlusion factor to darken it.

Code Example (Simplified)

OpenGL Shading Language

// ... in fragment shader ...

```glsl
float calculateAO(vec2 texCoord) {

  float occlusion = 0.0;

  for (int i = 0; i < numSamples; ++i) {

    // ... sample depth buffer at sample point ...

    if (sampledDepth < currentDepth) {

      occlusion += 1.0;

    }

  }

  return occlusion / numSamples;

}


void main() {

  // ... other calculations ...


  float ao = calculateAO(texCoord);

  fragColor = fragColor * (1.0 - ao);

}
```

Optimizations

- **Blurring:** Apply a blur filter to the occlusion map to smooth out noise and artifacts.
- **Noise Textures:** Use noise textures to randomize sample points and improve the quality of the occlusion.
- **Distance-Based Attenuation:** Attenuate the occlusion based on the distance between the sample point and the current pixel.
- **Efficient Sampling:** Utilize efficient sampling patterns and techniques to reduce the number of samples required.

Benefits of SSAO

- **Real-time Performance:** Approximates ambient occlusion efficiently, suitable for real-time applications.
- **Enhanced Realism:** Adds subtle shadows and depth to scenes, improving visual fidelity.
- **Easy Integration:** Can be easily integrated into existing rendering pipelines.

SSAO in Action

SSAO is widely used in games and 3D applications to enhance the realism of scenes without the computational cost of full ambient occlusion calculations. It adds a subtle but effective touch that improves the overall visual quality and immersion.

By understanding the principles and implementation of SSAO, you can add another valuable tool to your Vulkan rendering toolkit, enabling you to create more realistic and visually appealing 3D scenes.

Chapter 12: Vulkan Extensions and Portability

The Vulkan Ecosystem: Layers and Extensions

As a seasoned tech expert, you appreciate the balance Vulkan strikes between a core set of functionalities and the flexibility to adapt and evolve. This balance is achieved through a rich ecosystem of layers and extensions that augment the core Vulkan API, providing developers with tools for debugging, validation, and access to cutting-edge features.[1]

Layers: Enhancing Functionality and Control

Vulkan layers are optional components that act as intermediaries between your application and the Vulkan driver.[2] They can intercept Vulkan API calls, allowing them to:

- **Validate API Usage:** Identify incorrect or invalid API usage, helping you catch errors during development.[3]
- **Debug Applications:** Provide debugging information and assist in troubleshooting issues.[4]
- **Profile Performance:** Collect performance data and identify bottlenecks.[5]

- **Add Functionality:** Implement optional features or extensions that are not available in the core Vulkan API or the driver.[6]
- **Modify Behavior:** Modify the behavior of existing Vulkan functions, enabling custom functionality or workarounds.[7]

Types of Layers

- **Validation Layers:** Crucial for debugging, these layers check for API usage errors, ensuring your application adheres to the Vulkan specification.[8]
- **Debugging Layers:** Provide additional debugging information, such as API call tracing, object naming, and state inspection.
- **Profiling Layers:** Collect performance data, such as function timings and GPU counters, to identify performance bottlenecks.[9]
- **API Dump Layers:** Capture and log API calls, aiding in debugging and understanding application behavior.[10]
- **Synchronization Validation Layers:** Specifically validate synchronization primitives (semaphores, fences) to ensure correct usage and prevent data races.[11]

Enabling Layers

Layers are enabled during instance creation by specifying the desired layer names in the VkInstanceCreateInfo structure. The Vulkan loader then loads the specified layers and inserts them into the API call chain.[12]

Extensions: Expanding Vulkan's Capabilities

Vulkan extensions are optional additions to the core Vulkan API that provide access to:

- **New Hardware Features:** Expose new hardware capabilities, such as ray tracing, mesh shaders, or variable rate shading.
- **Platform-Specific Functionality:** Integrate with platform-specific APIs or features, such as windowing systems or operating system services.
- **Development Tools:** Support debugging, profiling, and other development tools.[13]
- **Community-Driven Features:** Introduce features driven by the Vulkan community, fostering innovation and collaboration.

Types of Extensions

- **Instance Extensions:** Extend the functionality of the Vulkan instance, such as querying available layers and extensions or creating surfaces.
- **Device Extensions:** Extend the capabilities of physical devices, such as supporting new

hardware features or providing access to specific device functionalities.[14]

Enabling Extensions

Extensions are enabled by specifying the desired extension names during instance or device creation.[15] The Vulkan loader then checks if the requested extensions are supported by the driver and enables them if available.

The Vulkan Registry

The Vulkan Registry is an online repository that maintains a comprehensive list of all available Vulkan extensions and their specifications.[16] It serves as a valuable resource for developers to explore and utilize the vast ecosystem of Vulkan extensions.

Benefits of Layers and Extensions

- **Flexibility:** Adapts to evolving hardware and software environments by providing access to new features and functionalities.[17]
- **Customization:** Allows developers to tailor Vulkan to their specific needs by enabling only the necessary layers and extensions.
- **Innovation:** Fosters innovation and community involvement by enabling the development and distribution of extensions.

- **Portability:** Promotes portability by providing a mechanism for accessing platform-specific features in a standardized way.[18]

By understanding the role of layers and extensions in the Vulkan ecosystem, you can effectively leverage their capabilities to enhance your development process, access cutting-edge features, and create portable and high-performance Vulkan applications.

Using Extensions for Advanced Features

As an experienced tech expert, you know that Vulkan's core API provides a solid foundation, but to access cutting-edge features and push the boundaries of graphics rendering, you need to tap into the vast landscape of Vulkan extensions. Extensions offer a mechanism to incorporate new hardware capabilities, platform-specific functionalities, and community-driven innovations, keeping your Vulkan applications at the forefront of graphics technology.

Accessing New Hardware Capabilities

GPU vendors are constantly pushing the boundaries of hardware capabilities, introducing new features that enable more realistic, efficient, and immersive graphics rendering. Vulkan extensions provide a standardized way to access these features, ensuring compatibility across different hardware implementations.

Examples of extensions that expose advanced hardware features:

- **VK_KHR_ray_tracing_pipeline:** Enables real-time ray tracing, allowing for accurate reflections, refractions, and global illumination effects.
- **VK_KHR_acceleration_structure:** Provides the building blocks for constructing acceleration structures, which are essential for efficient ray tracing.
- **VK_EXT_mesh_shader:** Introduces mesh shaders, a new shader stage that provides more flexibility and control over geometry processing.
- **VK_KHR_fragment_shading_rate:** Enables variable rate shading (VRS), allowing you to control the shading rate for different regions of the screen, optimizing performance and visual quality.

Integrating with Platform-Specific APIs

Vulkan extensions also facilitate integration with platform-specific APIs and services, enabling seamless interaction with the underlying operating system and windowing system.

Examples of extensions for platform integration:

- **VK_KHR_surface:** Provides a mechanism for creating Vulkan surfaces, which represent windows or displays where rendering output is presented.
- **VK_KHR_swapchain:** Enables the creation and management of swapchains, which are essential for smooth and tear-free rendering.
- **VK_EXT_debug_utils:** Provides a more robust and flexible way to debug Vulkan applications, including message logging and error reporting.

Exploring Community-Driven Features

The Vulkan community plays an active role in developing and proposing new extensions, fostering innovation and collaboration. These extensions often introduce experimental or specialized features that cater to specific needs or use cases.

Examples of community-driven extensions:

- **VK_EXT_transform_feedback:** Enables transform feedback, allowing you to capture the output of vertex processing for use in other computations or rendering techniques.
- **VK_EXT_conditional_rendering:** Provides a mechanism for conditional rendering, allowing

you to selectively render parts of the scene based on certain conditions.

- **VK_EXT_shader_image_atomic_int64:** Extends the capabilities of image atomics, enabling atomic operations on 64-bit integer values in shaders.

Keeping Up with Extensions

The Vulkan ecosystem is constantly evolving, with new extensions being introduced regularly. To stay up-to-date with the latest advancements:

- **Consult the Vulkan Registry:** Refer to the Vulkan Registry for a comprehensive list of available extensions and their specifications.
- **Follow Vulkan News:** Stay informed about new extensions and updates through Vulkan news sources and community forums.
- **Experiment and Explore:** Don't hesitate to experiment with new extensions and incorporate them into your applications to enhance functionality and performance.

By actively exploring and utilizing Vulkan extensions, you can unlock advanced features, integrate with platform-specific APIs, and tap into the innovative spirit of the Vulkan community. This allows you to create cutting-edge graphics applications that push the boundaries of visual fidelity and performance.

Cross-Platform Development Considerations

As an experienced tech expert with over two decades in the field, you know the allure of cross-platform development. Writing code once and deploying it across multiple operating systems (Windows, Linux, macOS) and even embedded systems can significantly reduce development time and effort. However, cross-platform development with Vulkan presents unique challenges that require careful consideration.

1. The Vulkan API: A Cross-Platform Foundation

While Vulkan itself is designed to be cross-platform, the surrounding ecosystem, including windowing systems, input handling, and platform-specific extensions, can introduce variations across different platforms.

2. Windowing System Integration

Each operating system has its own windowing system (Windows, X11, Wayland, macOS), and integrating with these systems requires platform-specific code. Libraries like GLFW or SDL can abstract away some of these differences, but you might still need to handle platform-specific nuances.

3. Input Handling

Handling user input, such as keyboard, mouse, and gamepad events, also involves platform-specific APIs. Again, libraries like GLFW or SDL can help, but be prepared to handle platform-specific variations.

4. Platform-Specific Extensions

Vulkan extensions can expose platform-specific features or functionalities. When using such extensions, you need to ensure they are available on the target platforms and provide fallback mechanisms or alternative implementations if they are not.

5. Shader Compiler Variations

Shader compilers can vary across platforms, potentially leading to different shader compilation behavior or performance characteristics. Test your shaders on different platforms to ensure consistent results.

6. Performance Considerations

While Vulkan offers a performance advantage on many platforms, performance characteristics can still vary across different hardware and driver implementations. Profile and optimize your application on each target platform to achieve the best possible performance.

7. Debugging and Validation

Debugging and validation tools can vary across platforms. Utilize platform-specific debugging tools and techniques when necessary to troubleshoot issues effectively.

8. Build Systems and Toolchains

Different platforms have different build systems and toolchains. Utilize cross-platform build systems like CMake to simplify the build process and ensure consistency across platforms.

9. Testing and Deployment

Thoroughly test your application on all target platforms to ensure compatibility and stability. Consider using continuous integration systems to automate the build and testing process.

10. Best Practices

- **Abstract Platform-Specific Code:** Isolate platform-specific code into separate modules or functions to improve maintainability and portability.
- **Utilize Cross-Platform Libraries:** Leverage cross-platform libraries like GLFW, SDL, or glm to handle windowing, input, and math operations.

- **Profile and Optimize per Platform:** Profile and optimize your application on each target platform to achieve the best possible performance.
- **Test Thoroughly:** Test your application on all target platforms to ensure compatibility and stability.

By carefully considering these cross-platform development factors and adopting best practices, you can successfully create Vulkan applications that run seamlessly across various platforms, expanding your reach and maximizing the impact of your work.

Future Directions of Vulkan

Given your extensive tech background, you understand that technology never stands still. Vulkan, despite its relative youth, continues to evolve, driven by advancements in hardware, the demands of emerging applications, and the collaborative efforts of the Khronos Group and the Vulkan community. Let's explore some of the key future directions that are shaping the landscape of Vulkan.

1. New Hardware Features

As GPU vendors push the boundaries of graphics technology, Vulkan needs to adapt to expose these new capabilities. We can expect to see extensions and API updates that support:

- **Ray Tracing Advancements:** Enhanced ray tracing features, such as more efficient acceleration structures, improved denoising techniques, and support for path tracing.
- **Mesh Shaders:** Wider adoption and refinement of mesh shaders, offering more flexibility and control over geometry processing.
- **Variable Rate Shading (VRS):** More sophisticated VRS techniques, allowing for finer-grained control over shading rates and improved performance optimization.
- **Machine Learning Integration:** Closer integration with machine learning hardware and software, enabling hardware-accelerated AI inference and training within Vulkan applications.

2. Cross-Platform Evolution

Vulkan's cross-platform nature is a key strength, and we can expect continued efforts to improve portability and support a wider range of platforms:

- **Mobile and Embedded Devices:** Enhanced support for mobile and embedded GPUs, enabling high-performance graphics on resource-constrained devices.

- **WebGPU Integration:** Closer alignment with the WebGPU standard, facilitating the development of high-performance graphics applications for the web.
- **Integration with Other APIs:** Improved interoperability with other graphics APIs, such as DirectX 12 and Metal, enabling developers to leverage Vulkan's strengths within diverse ecosystems.

3. Developer Experience

The Vulkan API, while powerful, can be complex to learn and use. Future developments are likely to focus on improving the developer experience:

- **Simplified API:** Higher-level abstractions and helper libraries to simplify common tasks and reduce boilerplate code.
- **Enhanced Tools:** More robust debugging, profiling, and validation tools to aid in development and optimization.
- **Improved Documentation and Tutorials:** Clearer and more comprehensive documentation and tutorials to facilitate learning and adoption.

4. Community Involvement

The Vulkan community plays a vital role in shaping the future of the API. We can expect continued community involvement through:

- **Open-Source Projects:** Development of open-source tools, libraries, and frameworks that enhance the Vulkan ecosystem.
- **Feedback and Collaboration:** Active participation in feedback channels and collaborative efforts to influence the direction of Vulkan's evolution.
- **Extension Development:** Community-driven development of extensions that introduce new features or address specific needs.

5. Efficiency and Performance

Vulkan's focus on efficiency and performance will remain a driving force:

- **Reduced Overhead:** Ongoing efforts to minimize API overhead and improve driver efficiency.
- **Enhanced Concurrency:** Better support for multi-threading and asynchronous compute to maximize GPU utilization.
- **Power Optimization:** Techniques and features to reduce power consumption, especially on mobile and embedded devices.

Staying Ahead of the Curve

As Vulkan continues to evolve, it's essential to stay informed about the latest developments and adapt your skills and knowledge accordingly:

- **Follow Vulkan News:** Keep up with news and announcements from the Khronos Group and other Vulkan sources.
- **Engage with the Community:** Participate in online forums and discussions to share knowledge and learn from others.
- **Experiment with New Features:** Explore new extensions and features as they become available to expand your Vulkan capabilities.

By staying informed and engaged with the Vulkan ecosystem, you can position yourself at the forefront of graphics technology, leveraging the latest advancements to create innovative and high-performance applications.

Part IV: Building Real-World Applications

Chapter 13: Building a Simple Game Engine

Engine Architecture and Design

As a seasoned tech expert with a wealth of experience, you understand that game engines are the powerhouses behind interactive experiences, providing the framework and tools for creating immersive virtual worlds. Designing a game engine, even a simple one, involves careful consideration of its architecture and the interplay of its various components. Let's explore the key elements that contribute to a robust and efficient game engine design.

Core Components

A game engine typically comprises several core components that work in concert to bring your game to life:

- **Core Systems:**
    - **Initialization and Shutdown:** Handles engine startup and shutdown procedures, including resource loading and memory management.
    - **Main Loop:** Drives the game's execution, updating game state, processing input,

and rendering frames in a continuous cycle.

- ○ **Resource Management:** Provides efficient loading, storage, and access to game assets such as textures, meshes, and sounds.
- ○ **Logging and Debugging:** Facilitates debugging and error tracking by providing logging mechanisms and diagnostic tools.
- **Graphics:**
  - ○ **Rendering Engine:** Handles the rendering of 3D scenes, including shader management, pipeline creation, and draw call optimization.
  - ○ **Scene Management:** Organizes and manages the scene graph, including object hierarchies, transformations, and rendering order.
  - ○ **Camera System:** Controls the camera's position, orientation, and projection, defining the player's view of the world.
- **Input:**
  - ○ **Input Handling:** Processes user input from various devices, such as keyboard, mouse, and gamepad.

- o **Event System:** Distributes input events to relevant game objects or systems for processing.
- **Game Logic:**
  - o **Game Object System:** Provides a framework for creating and managing game objects, including their components, behaviors, and interactions.
  - o **Physics Engine (Optional):** Simulates realistic physics interactions, such as collisions, gravity, and rigid body dynamics.
  - o **AI System (Optional):** Implements artificial intelligence for non-player characters (NPCs), enabling intelligent behavior and decision-making.
- **Audio:**
  - o **Audio Engine:** Handles sound playback, mixing, and spatialization.
  - o **Sound Management:** Provides loading and management of sound assets.

Architectural Considerations

- **Modularity:** Design the engine with modularity in mind, separating functionalities into distinct components or modules. This promotes code reusability, maintainability, and extensibility.

- **Abstraction:** Abstract away platform-specific details and hardware complexities to improve portability and simplify development.
- **Data-Driven Design:** Utilize data-driven approaches to store and manage game content, allowing for easy modification and customization without recompiling code.
- **Performance:** Prioritize performance optimization throughout the engine's design, considering factors like memory management, draw call optimization, and efficient algorithms.

Design Patterns

Consider employing common design patterns to improve the structure and flexibility of your engine:

- **Component-Based Architecture:** Break down game objects into reusable components, promoting modularity and code reuse.
- **Observer Pattern:** Implement an event system to decouple communication between different engine components.
- **Singleton Pattern:** Use singletons for managing global resources or systems that require a single point of access.
- **Factory Pattern:** Create objects through factory methods to abstract away creation logic and improve flexibility.

Tools and Libraries

Leverage existing tools and libraries to accelerate development and avoid reinventing the wheel:

- **Graphics Libraries:** Utilize Vulkan for rendering, GLFW or SDL for windowing and input handling, and glm for math operations.
- **Physics Engines:** Consider integrating physics engines like Bullet or PhysX for realistic physics simulations.
- **Audio Libraries:** Use audio libraries like OpenAL or FMOD for sound playback and management.

Iterative Development

Develop your game engine iteratively, starting with a basic framework and gradually adding features and functionalities. This allows you to test and refine the engine as you progress, ensuring stability and maintainability.

By carefully considering these architectural and design principles, you can lay a solid foundation for a simple yet robust game engine. This engine can then serve as a platform for creating interactive experiences, exploring game development concepts, and unleashing your creativity in the realm of virtual worlds.

Resource Management

Given your extensive tech expertise, you know that game development often involves handling a vast array of assets, from textures and meshes to sounds and scripts. Efficient resource management is crucial for ensuring smooth loading, optimal memory usage, and a seamless gameplay experience. Let's explore the key aspects of resource management in your Vulkan game engine.

1. Resource Types

Identify the types of resources your engine will handle:

- **Textures:** Images used for visual representation, including diffuse maps, normal maps, and environment maps.
- **Meshes:** 3D models composed of vertices and faces, defining the shape of objects in the game world.
- **Shaders:** Programs that run on the GPU, responsible for transforming and shading geometry.
- **Sounds:** Audio files used for sound effects, music, and ambient sounds.
- **Scripts:** Code files that define game logic, behavior, and interactions.
- **Fonts:** Typeface data used for rendering text.

- **Animation Data:** Data that describes skeletal animations or other animation sequences.
- **Configuration Files:** Data files that store game settings, preferences, or level data.

2. Loading and Storage

Implement mechanisms for efficiently loading and storing resources:

- **Asynchronous Loading:** Load resources asynchronously to avoid blocking the main thread and ensure smooth gameplay.
- **Caching:** Cache frequently used resources in memory to reduce loading times and improve performance.
- **Compression:** Compress large resources to reduce memory footprint and loading times.
- **Serialization:** Serialize and deserialize resources to store them on disk or transmit them over a network.
- **File Formats:** Support various file formats for different resource types, using libraries or custom parsers.

3. Resource Handling

Develop strategies for managing resources during gameplay:

- **Reference Counting:** Keep track of resource usage through reference counting to ensure proper memory management and avoid leaks.
- **Garbage Collection:** Implement a garbage collection mechanism to automatically reclaim unused resources.
- **Resource Lifetime:** Manage the lifetime of resources, unloading or releasing them when they are no longer needed.
- **Streaming:** For large or dynamic worlds, implement resource streaming to load and unload resources as the player moves through the environment.

4. API Design

Design a clear and consistent API for accessing and managing resources:

- **Resource Handles:** Use resource handles (e.g., IDs or pointers) to abstract away resource loading and management details.
- **Resource Managers:** Create resource managers for different resource types to encapsulate loading, storage, and access logic.
- **Asynchronous Operations:** Provide asynchronous functions for loading and processing resources, allowing for non-blocking operations.

5. Tools and Libraries

Leverage existing tools and libraries to simplify resource management:

- **Asset Management Systems:** Consider using asset management systems to organize, track, and import game assets.
- **Serialization Libraries:** Utilize libraries like JSON or XML parsers for serializing and deserializing data.
- **Compression Libraries:** Use libraries like zlib or LZ4 for compressing and decompressing resources.

6. Optimizations

Optimize resource management for performance:

- **Reduce Disk I/O:** Minimize disk access by caching and compressing resources.
- **Memory Pooling:** Use memory pooling to avoid frequent memory allocations and deallocations.
- **Batch Loading:** Combine multiple resource loading requests into batches to reduce overhead.

7. Memory Management

Integrate resource management with Vulkan's memory management capabilities:

- **Dedicated Allocations:** Allocate dedicated memory for large resources to avoid fragmentation and improve performance.
- **Staging Buffers:** Use staging buffers for efficient transfer of resource data to device-local memory.
- **Sparse Memory:** Consider using sparse memory for very large resources to optimize memory usage.

By implementing efficient resource management strategies and utilizing appropriate tools and libraries, you can ensure that your Vulkan game engine handles assets effectively. This contributes to smooth loading times, optimal memory usage, and a seamless gameplay experience for your players.

Input Handling and Game Loop

As an experienced tech expert, you know that games are not merely about rendering visuals; they thrive on interaction and responsiveness. Input handling and the game loop are essential components of your Vulkan game engine, capturing player actions and translating them into meaningful events within the game world.

Input Handling: Capturing Player Intent

Input handling involves capturing player actions from various devices, such as:

- **Keyboard:** Key presses and releases.
- **Mouse:** Movement, button clicks, and scrolling.
- **Gamepad:** Button presses, joystick movements, and trigger activations.
- **Touchscreen:** Touches, taps, and gestures.

Input Handling Strategies

- **Polling:** Periodically check the state of input devices to detect changes.
- **Events:** Receive notifications (events) when input actions occur.

Implementing Input Handling in Vulkan

1. **Platform-Specific APIs:** Utilize platform-specific APIs or libraries (e.g., GLFW, SDL) to access input device data.
2. **Abstraction Layer:** Create an abstraction layer to handle platform-specific variations and provide a consistent input API for your engine.
3. **Input Mapping:** Allow users to customize input mappings to suit their preferences.
4. **Event System:** Distribute input events to relevant game objects or systems for processing.

The Game Loop: Driving the Interactive Experience

The game loop is the central driving force of your game, responsible for continuously updating the game state and rendering frames. It typically follows this structure:

1. **Process Input:** Capture and handle player input, translating actions into game events.
2. **Update Game Logic:** Update the state of the game world, including object positions, physics simulations, AI behaviors, and game logic.
3. **Render Frame:** Render the current state of the game world to the screen, utilizing Vulkan's rendering capabilities.

Game Loop Variations

- **Fixed Timestep:** Update game logic at a fixed rate, ensuring consistent behavior regardless of frame rate.
- **Variable Timestep:** Update game logic based on the time elapsed since the last frame, allowing for smoother animation and responsiveness.
- **Delta Time:** Use delta time (the time elapsed since the last frame) in calculations to ensure consistent behavior across different frame rates.

Code Example (Simplified)

C++

```
while (!windowShouldClose) {
```

```
// Process input

processInput();


// Update game logic

updateGame(deltaTime);


// Render frame

renderFrame();
}
```

Optimizations

- **Input Queuing:** Queue input events to avoid losing input data between frames.
- **Multithreading:** Utilize multithreading to perform input handling, game logic updates, and rendering in parallel, improving performance.
- **Time Budgeting:** Allocate specific time budgets for different parts of the game loop to ensure consistent frame rates and avoid performance spikes.

Input Handling and Game Loop in Action

The combination of input handling and the game loop creates the interactive heartbeat of your game. It captures player actions, translates them into meaningful events, and drives the dynamic evolution of the game world.

By implementing robust input handling and a well-structured game loop, you can create responsive and engaging gameplay experiences in your Vulkan game engine, ensuring that players feel connected to the virtual worlds you create.

Integrating Physics and Collision Detection

As an experienced tech expert, you know that realistic physics interactions can greatly enhance the immersion and engagement of your games. Integrating a physics engine into your Vulkan game engine allows you to simulate realistic object movements, collisions, and other physical phenomena, creating a more believable and interactive experience for your players.

Choosing a Physics Engine

Several popular physics engines are available for integration into game engines:

- **Bullet Physics:** An open-source, widely used physics engine known for its stability and performance.

- **PhysX:** A robust physics engine developed by NVIDIA, offering a comprehensive set of features and GPU acceleration capabilities.
- **Box2D:** A 2D physics engine well-suited for side-scrolling or top-down games.

Integration Strategies

Integrating a physics engine involves establishing communication between the physics engine and your game engine:

1. **Data Exchange:** Exchange data between the physics engine and your game engine, including object positions, rotations, velocities, and collision information.
2. **Synchronization:** Synchronize the physics simulation with the game loop, ensuring that physics updates occur at the appropriate timesteps.
3. **Collision Detection:** Utilize the physics engine's collision detection capabilities to detect collisions between objects in the game world.
4. **Collision Response:** Implement collision response logic to handle collisions appropriately, such as applying forces, triggering events, or modifying object behavior.

Key Concepts in Physics Simulation

- **Rigid Bodies:** Objects that maintain their shape and do not deform under forces.
- **Collision Shapes:** Geometric representations of objects used for collision detection.
- **Constraints:** Restrictions on the movement or behavior of objects, such as joints or hinges.
- **Forces:** Influences that cause objects to accelerate or change their motion.

Collision Detection Techniques

Physics engines employ various collision detection techniques, including:

- **Bounding Volume Hierarchies (BVHs):** Hierarchical structures that partition the scene to accelerate collision detection.
- **Shape Casting:** Casting rays or shapes into the scene to detect collisions.
- **Contact Manifolds:** Detailed information about contact points between colliding objects.

Implementing Collision Response

Collision response logic determines how objects react to collisions:

- **Impulse-Based Resolution:** Apply impulses (instantaneous forces) to resolve collisions and prevent objects from interpenetrating.

- **Constraint-Based Resolution:** Use constraints to maintain physical relationships between objects, such as preventing them from separating or exceeding certain limits.
- **Event Triggers:** Trigger game events based on collisions, such as playing sounds, inflicting damage, or changing object states.

Optimizations

- **Fixed Timestep:** Use a fixed timestep for the physics simulation to ensure consistent behavior.
- **Substepping:** Subdivide the physics timestep into smaller steps for more accurate simulations.
- **Asynchronous Physics:** Perform physics updates on a separate thread to avoid blocking the main thread.
- **Collision Layers and Masks:** Use collision layers and masks to selectively control which objects collide with each other.

Physics and Collision Detection in Action

Integrating physics and collision detection brings a level of realism and interactivity to your games that enhances the gameplay experience. Objects move and interact in a believable manner, collisions feel impactful, and players can engage with the game world in a more immersive way.

By incorporating a physics engine and implementing collision detection and response, you can create dynamic and engaging gameplay scenarios, adding another layer of depth and realism to your Vulkan game engine.

Chapter 14: Creating a 3D Visualization Tool

Data Loading and Processing

As an experienced tech expert, you know that 3D visualization tools are essential for understanding and analyzing complex datasets. Whether you're visualizing scientific data, medical scans, or financial models, the ability to load and process data efficiently is crucial for creating meaningful and interactive visualizations.

1. Data Sources and Formats

Identify the types of data your visualization tool will handle:

- **Scientific Data:** Simulation outputs, sensor readings, experimental results, often stored in formats like CSV, HDF5, or NetCDF.
- **Medical Imaging:** CT scans, MRI scans, ultrasound images, typically stored in DICOM or NIfTI formats.
- **Geographic Data:** Terrain data, elevation models, satellite imagery, often found in formats like GeoTIFF or Shapefile.
- **Financial Data:** Stock prices, market trends, economic indicators, commonly stored in CSV or databases.

- **Engineering Models:** CAD models, structural analysis data, typically stored in formats like STEP or IGES.

2. Data Loading

Implement robust data loading mechanisms:

- **File Parsers:** Develop or utilize libraries to parse various data formats, extracting relevant information for visualization.
- **Database Connections:** Establish connections to databases to retrieve and visualize data stored in relational or NoSQL databases.
- **Network Communication:** Implement network protocols to load data from remote servers or cloud storage.
- **Asynchronous Loading:** Load large datasets asynchronously to avoid blocking the main thread and maintain responsiveness.
- **Progress Indicators:** Provide feedback to the user about the loading progress for large datasets.

3. Data Processing

Transform and prepare the loaded data for visualization:

- **Data Cleaning:** Handle missing or erroneous data, ensuring data integrity and accuracy.

- **Normalization:** Scale data values to a specific range for consistent visualization.
- **Filtering:** Filter data based on user-defined criteria to focus on specific aspects of the dataset.
- **Interpolation:** Interpolate data to generate smooth transitions or fill in missing values.
- **Data Reduction:** Reduce the size of large datasets through techniques like decimation or sampling to improve performance.

4. Data Structures

Choose appropriate data structures to represent the processed data:

- **Point Clouds:** Represent data as a collection of points with associated attributes.
- **Meshes:** Convert point clouds or volumetric data into meshes for surface rendering.
- **Volumetric Grids:** Represent 3D data as a grid of values, enabling volumetric rendering techniques.
- **Graphs and Networks:** Visualize relationships between data points as graphs or networks.

5. Vulkan Integration

Integrate data loading and processing with Vulkan's rendering capabilities:

- **Vertex Buffers:** Store processed data in vertex buffers for efficient rendering.
- **Texture Buffers:** Utilize texture buffers to store and access large datasets in shaders.
- **Storage Buffers:** Employ storage buffers for dynamic data updates and interaction with compute shaders.

6. Optimizations

Optimize data loading and processing for performance:

- **Multithreading:** Utilize multithreading to parallelize data loading and processing tasks.
- **GPU Acceleration:** Offload data processing tasks to the GPU using compute shaders.
- **Data Caching:** Cache frequently accessed data to reduce redundant computations.
- **Memory Management:** Efficiently manage memory usage to avoid bottlenecks and improve performance.

7. User Interaction

Allow users to interact with the visualized data:

- **Data Selection:** Enable users to select and highlight specific data points or regions.

- **Data Manipulation:** Provide tools for manipulating the data, such as filtering, slicing, or zooming.
- **Animation:** Animate data over time to visualize dynamic processes or trends.

By implementing robust data loading and processing techniques and integrating them with Vulkan's rendering capabilities, you can create powerful 3D visualization tools that provide valuable insights into complex datasets. These tools empower users to explore, analyze, and understand data in new and interactive ways, facilitating scientific discovery, medical diagnosis, and informed decision-making.

Interactive Controls and Camera Movement

As a seasoned tech expert, you understand that effective 3D visualization tools require intuitive controls that allow users to seamlessly navigate and interact with the visualized data. Implementing interactive controls and camera movement is crucial for enabling users to explore the 3D scene, focus on areas of interest, and gain a comprehensive understanding of the data.

1. Input Handling

Start by establishing robust input handling mechanisms:

- **Keyboard Input:** Process keyboard events to trigger actions like rotation, translation, zooming, or data manipulation.
- **Mouse Input:** Utilize mouse movement and button clicks for camera control, object selection, and interaction with UI elements.
- **Gamepad Support:** Consider adding support for gamepads to provide an alternative input method, especially for immersive or VR-based visualizations.

2. Camera Control

Implement various camera control modes:

- **Orbit:** Rotate the camera around a target point, allowing users to examine the data from different angles.
- **Pan:** Translate the camera horizontally and vertically, enabling users to explore the scene.
- **Zoom:** Move the camera closer to or farther from the target point, allowing users to adjust the level of detail.
- **First-Person:** Provide a first-person camera mode for immersive exploration of the data, especially for architectural or environmental visualizations.

3. Navigation Techniques

Implement intuitive navigation techniques:

- **Mouse Look:** Use mouse movement to control the camera's orientation, providing a natural and intuitive way to look around the scene.
- **WASD Movement:** Utilize the WASD keys for first-person movement, allowing users to walk or fly through the 3D environment.
- **Scroll Wheel Zoom:** Use the scroll wheel for zooming in and out, providing a familiar and convenient way to adjust the view.

4. Object Interaction

Enable users to interact with visualized objects:

- **Selection:** Allow users to select objects using mouse clicks or ray casting techniques.
- **Highlighting:** Highlight selected objects to provide visual feedback.
- **Manipulation:** Enable users to translate, rotate, or scale selected objects to explore their structure or relationships.

5. UI Integration

Integrate interactive controls with the user interface:

- **GUI Controls:** Provide GUI elements (buttons, sliders, etc.) to adjust camera parameters, control visualization settings, or trigger actions.

- **On-Screen Overlays:** Display on-screen overlays to provide information about selected objects or guide user interaction.

6. Optimizations

Optimize camera movement and interaction for smooth and responsive performance:

- **Frame Rate Independence:** Decouple camera movement and interaction from the frame rate to ensure consistent behavior across different hardware configurations.
- **Input Smoothing:** Smooth out camera movement and input to avoid jerky or abrupt transitions.
- **Collision Detection:** Prevent the camera from moving through objects or exceeding scene boundaries.

7. Advanced Interactions

Consider implementing advanced interaction techniques:

- **Virtual Reality (VR):** Integrate VR support to provide immersive and interactive data exploration experiences.
- **Augmented Reality (AR):** Overlay visualizations onto the real world using AR technologies.

- **Gesture Recognition:** Utilize gesture recognition to control the camera or interact with data using hand movements.

By implementing intuitive interactive controls and camera movement, you can empower users to navigate and explore the 3D visualization with ease. This enhances their understanding of the data, facilitates exploration of complex structures, and promotes engagement with the visualized information.

Visualizing Scientific and Engineering Data

Given your extensive tech expertise, you recognize the indispensable role of 3D visualization in scientific and engineering domains. It transforms complex datasets, intricate simulations, and abstract concepts into tangible visual representations, facilitating analysis, communication, and discovery. Let's explore the key aspects of creating effective 3D visualization tools for scientific and engineering data using Vulkan.

1. Understanding the Data

Begin by understanding the nature and structure of the data you'll be visualizing:

- **Types of Data:**

- Scalar Fields: Represent a single value at each point in space, such as temperature, pressure, or density.
- Vector Fields: Represent magnitude and direction at each point, such as velocity, force, or flow.
- Tensor Fields: Represent multi-dimensional values at each point, such as stress or strain in a material.
- Time-Varying Data: Data that changes over time, such as simulations or dynamic processes.
- Multi-Dimensional Data: Data with more than three dimensions, requiring techniques like dimensionality reduction or slicing to visualize.

2. Visualization Techniques

Employ appropriate visualization techniques to represent the data effectively:

- **Scalar Field Visualization:**
  - **Color Mapping:** Map scalar values to colors to represent variations in the field.
  - **Isosurfaces:** Extract surfaces of constant value (isosurfaces) to visualize boundaries or regions of interest.

- **Volume Rendering:** Render the volume directly, revealing internal structures and variations.
- **Vector Field Visualization:**
  - **Glyphs:** Use arrows or other glyphs to represent vectors at different points in the field.
  - **Streamlines:** Trace the paths of particles through the vector field to visualize flow patterns.
  - **Line Integral Convolution (LIC):** Create textured representations of vector fields to visualize complex flow patterns.
- **Mesh Visualization:**
  - **Surface Rendering:** Render the surfaces of 3D meshes, applying lighting and shading for visual appeal.
  - **Wireframe Rendering:** Display the edges of the mesh to highlight its structure.
  - **Cross-sections:** Slice through the mesh to reveal internal details.

3. Vulkan Implementation

Leverage Vulkan's capabilities for efficient and high-quality rendering:

- **Vertex Buffers:** Store data points or mesh vertices in vertex buffers for efficient rendering.
- **Shaders:** Implement visualization techniques and data manipulation in shaders for flexibility and performance.
- **Textures:** Utilize textures for color mapping, volume rendering, or storing data attributes.
- **Compute Shaders:** Offload data processing or visualization tasks to the GPU using compute shaders.

4. Interaction and Exploration

Provide interactive tools for users to explore and analyze the data:

- **Camera Control:** Allow users to navigate the 3D scene using various camera controls (orbit, pan, zoom).
- **Data Selection:** Enable users to select and highlight specific data points or regions of interest.
- **Data Manipulation:** Provide tools for filtering, slicing, or animating the data to focus on specific aspects.
- **Measurement Tools:** Implement measurement tools to quantify distances, angles, or other properties of the visualized data.

5. Examples in Scientific and Engineering Domains

- **Fluid Dynamics:** Visualize fluid flow simulations, showing pressure, velocity, and vorticity.
- **Structural Analysis:** Display stress and strain distributions in structures under load.
- **Medical Imaging:** Render 3D models of organs or tissues from medical scans, aiding in diagnosis and treatment planning.
- **Climate Modeling:** Visualize climate patterns, temperature variations, and other atmospheric data.
- **Molecular Dynamics:** Represent molecular structures and interactions in 3D.

By combining your deep understanding of technology with the principles of scientific and engineering visualization, you can create powerful tools that unlock insights hidden within complex datasets. These tools empower researchers, engineers, and scientists to make new discoveries, communicate their findings effectively, and advance knowledge in their respective fields.

Chapter 15: Developing a Virtual Reality Experience

VR Fundamentals and Headsets

With your extensive tech background, you recognize the transformative potential of virtual reality (VR) to create immersive and engaging experiences. Developing for VR involves understanding the fundamental principles that underpin this technology and the hardware that brings it to life. Let's explore the core concepts and the diverse landscape of VR headsets.

Fundamentals of VR

VR aims to create a sense of presence in a virtual environment by stimulating the user's senses and providing a convincing illusion of being physically present in a digital world. Key elements that contribute to this illusion include:

- **Stereoscopic Display:** Presenting slightly different images to each eye, creating the perception of depth and three-dimensionality.
- **Head Tracking:** Tracking the user's head movements and updating the displayed images accordingly, maintaining the illusion of spatial presence.

- **Motion Tracking (Optional):** Tracking the user's body movements, allowing for interaction with the virtual environment through physical actions.
- **Spatial Audio:** Providing 3D audio that simulates the way sound behaves in the real world, enhancing immersion and spatial awareness.
- **Interaction:** Enabling user interaction with the virtual environment through controllers, hand tracking, or other input devices.

Types of VR Headsets

VR headsets can be broadly categorized into several types:

- **PC VR:** High-end headsets that connect to a powerful PC to deliver high-fidelity visuals and immersive experiences.
  - Examples: Valve Index, HTC Vive Pro, Varjo Aero
- **Standalone VR:** All-in-one headsets that don't require a PC or external sensors, offering portability and ease of use.
  - Examples: Meta Quest 2, Pico 4, HTC Vive Focus 3

- **Mobile VR:** Headsets that utilize a smartphone as the display and processing unit, providing a more affordable entry point to VR.
  - Examples: Google Cardboard, Samsung Gear VR (discontinued)
- **Console VR:** Headsets designed specifically for gaming consoles, offering a balance between performance and affordability.
  - Example: PlayStation VR2

Key Headset Components

VR headsets typically consist of several key components:

- **Display:** Provides the visual experience, typically using LCD or OLED panels with high refresh rates and low persistence to minimize motion blur.
- **Lenses:** Focus and magnify the display image, creating the stereoscopic effect and immersive field of view.
- **Sensors:** Track the user's head movements (and potentially body movements) using various technologies like accelerometers, gyroscopes, and cameras.
- **Audio:** Integrated headphones or spatial audio systems to deliver immersive sound.

- **Input:** Controllers or hand tracking systems to enable interaction with the virtual environment.

Choosing a VR Headset

The choice of VR headset depends on several factors:

- **Budget:** Headsets range in price from affordable mobile VR options to high-end PC VR systems.
- **Platform:** Consider compatibility with your existing gaming PC or console, or opt for a standalone headset for portability.
- **Content:** Explore the available content and experiences for different platforms to ensure it aligns with your interests.
- **Technical Specifications:** Compare display resolution, refresh rate, field of view, tracking accuracy, and comfort features to find the best fit.

The Future of VR Headsets

VR technology is constantly evolving, and we can expect future headsets to offer:

- **Higher Resolutions and Refresh Rates:** Sharper visuals and smoother experiences.
- **Wider Fields of View:** More immersive and realistic sense of presence.
- **Improved Tracking:** More accurate and reliable tracking of head and body movements.

- **Enhanced Comfort:** Lighter and more comfortable designs for extended use.
- **Eye Tracking and Foveated Rendering:** Optimizing rendering by focusing processing power on the areas where the user is looking.
- **Wireless Connectivity:** Untethered experiences with wireless streaming or standalone capabilities.

By understanding the fundamentals of VR and the diverse landscape of VR headsets, you can make informed decisions about your development platform and create immersive experiences that transport users to new and exciting virtual worlds.

Rendering for VR: Stereo Images and Head Tracking

Given your tech expertise, you know that rendering for VR involves specific considerations to create a convincing and comfortable experience. The core of VR rendering lies in generating stereo images and seamlessly integrating head tracking to maintain the illusion of spatial presence.

Stereo Rendering: Two Perspectives, One World

Human vision perceives depth through the slightly different images each eye captures. VR replicates this by rendering two separate images, one for each eye, from slightly offset viewpoints. This creates the stereoscopic effect, tricking the brain into perceiving depth and three-dimensionality.

Key Steps in Stereo Rendering

1. **Calculate Eye Positions:** Determine the position of each eye based on the interpupillary distance (IPD), which is the distance between the user's eyes.
2. **Render Separate Views:** Render the scene twice, once for each eye, using the corresponding eye position as the viewpoint for the camera.
3. **Distortion Correction:** Apply distortion correction to the rendered images to compensate for the lenses in the VR headset, ensuring proper alignment and minimizing visual artifacts.
4. **Present to Headset:** Present the corrected images to the respective displays of the VR headset.

Vulkan and Stereo Rendering

Vulkan provides mechanisms for stereo rendering through extensions like VK_KHR_multiview or by rendering to separate framebuffers for each eye. The choice depends on the specific VR platform and hardware capabilities.

Head Tracking: Seamlessly Updating the View

Head tracking is crucial for maintaining the illusion of presence in VR. As the user moves their head, the rendered images must update accordingly to reflect the changing viewpoint. This requires continuous tracking of the user's head orientation and position.

Head Tracking Technologies

VR headsets utilize various technologies for head tracking:

- **Inertial Measurement Units (IMUs):** Sensors like accelerometers and gyroscopes measure head orientation and movement.
- **Cameras and Sensors:** External cameras or sensors track the headset's position and orientation in the physical space.
- **Inside-Out Tracking:** Cameras and sensors built into the headset track the surrounding environment to determine its position and movement.

Integrating Head Tracking into Rendering

1. **Obtain Tracking Data:** Retrieve the latest head tracking data from the VR platform or SDK.
2. **Update Camera Transformation:** Apply the head tracking data to the camera's transformation

matrix, adjusting its position and orientation in the virtual world.

3. **Render New Frames:** Render new frames with the updated camera transformation, reflecting the user's current head position and orientation.

Optimizations

- **Prediction:** Predict future head movements to reduce latency and improve responsiveness.
- **Asynchronous Timewarp:** Adjust the rendered images based on the latest head tracking data just before displaying them, minimizing motion blur and judder.
- **Late Latching:** Utilize the most recent head tracking data available when submitting frames to the GPU, further reducing latency.

Stereo Rendering and Head Tracking in Action

The combination of stereo rendering and head tracking creates the foundation for immersive VR experiences. By presenting two slightly different images to each eye and seamlessly updating the view based on head movements, VR applications can convincingly transport users into virtual worlds, allowing them to explore and interact with digital environments as if they were truly present.

Creating Immersive and Interactive VR Applications

As an experienced tech expert, you know that virtual reality (VR) offers more than just visual immersion; it's about engaging all the senses to create a truly compelling and believable experience. Building upon the foundation of stereo rendering and head tracking, let's explore the key elements that contribute to immersive and interactive VR applications.

1. Presence and Immersion

The sense of presence, the feeling of "being there" in the virtual environment, is paramount in VR. To enhance presence:

- **High-Fidelity Visuals:** Utilize high-resolution displays, realistic rendering techniques, and detailed environments to create a visually convincing world.
- **Spatial Audio:** Implement 3D audio that accurately simulates the way sound behaves in the real world, providing directional cues and enhancing immersion.
- **Comfortable Ergonomics:** Minimize discomfort and motion sickness by ensuring smooth frame rates, low latency, and comfortable headset design.

2. Interaction and Agency

Empowering users to interact with the virtual environment is crucial for engagement. Provide natural and intuitive ways for users to:

- **Manipulate Objects:** Allow users to pick up, move, and interact with virtual objects using controllers or hand tracking.
- **Navigate the Environment:** Implement comfortable and intuitive movement systems, such as teleportation, smooth locomotion, or room-scale tracking.
- **Perform Actions:** Enable users to perform actions within the virtual world, such as opening doors, pressing buttons, or interacting with characters.

3. Sensory Feedback

Consider incorporating additional sensory feedback to enhance immersion:

- **Haptic Feedback:** Use haptic devices to provide tactile sensations, such as vibrations or resistance, when interacting with objects.
- **Motion Platforms:** Employ motion platforms to simulate physical movement and enhance the sense of presence in dynamic scenarios.

4. Content and Experience

The content and experience you create are paramount to a successful VR application:

- **Compelling Narratives:** Craft engaging stories and experiences that draw users into the virtual world.
- **Interactive Environments:** Design interactive environments that encourage exploration and discovery.
- **Meaningful Interactions:** Provide meaningful interactions that give users a sense of agency and purpose within the virtual world.

5. Performance Optimization

Maintaining high frame rates and low latency is crucial for a comfortable VR experience. Optimize your application for performance:

- **Efficient Rendering:** Utilize rendering techniques like instancing, culling, and level of detail to minimize the rendering workload.
- **Asynchronous Operations:** Perform tasks like physics simulations or data loading asynchronously to avoid blocking the main thread.

- **Shader Optimization:** Optimize shader code to reduce computational complexity and improve rendering efficiency.

6. User Comfort

Prioritize user comfort to minimize motion sickness and fatigue:

- **Smooth Frame Rates:** Maintain consistent and high frame rates to avoid judder and disorientation.
- **Low Latency:** Minimize latency between head movements and visual updates to reduce motion sickness.
- **Comfortable Design:** Ensure the VR headset is comfortable to wear for extended periods.

7. Examples of Immersive VR Applications

- **Gaming:** Immersive first-person experiences, simulations, and interactive narratives.
- **Training and Education:** Simulate real-world scenarios for training purposes or create interactive educational experiences.
- **Design and Visualization:** Visualize architectural designs, explore 3D models, or experience virtual prototypes.

- **Therapy and Healthcare:** Utilize VR for exposure therapy, pain management, or rehabilitation exercises.

By combining your technical expertise with a focus on user experience and immersion, you can create compelling VR applications that engage the senses, transport users to new worlds, and unlock the full potential of this transformative technology.